# HERBAL TEA FOR BEGINNERS

*The Art of Herbal Infusions:*
*Simple Techniques for Making Perfect Herbal Tea*

## LUCY ABBOTT

# Table of Contents

# Introduction

## The growing popularity of herbal tea

In recent years, herbal tea has experienced a spectacular rise in popularity, catching the interest of both tea enthusiasts and health-conscious people. Herbal tea has become a popular beverage as people look for natural and holistic ways to improve their health. It offers enticing flavors in addition to a number of potential health advantages. In this section, we'll dig into the factors that have influenced herbal tea's widespread adoption as well as the reasons that have led to its rising popularity.

Herbal tea, commonly referred to as tisanes, has been consumed for its therapeutic benefits by many cultures for ages. The rise of herbal tea has been greatly influenced by the resurgence of interest in herbal medicines and conventional medicinal methods. Herbal tea is increasingly being used by people as a natural and holistic alternative to synthetic medications and artificial additives.

Herbal tea has entered the mainstream as a result of the rising emphasis on health and wellness. Herbal tea, in contrast to traditional teas like black or green tea, is naturally caffeine-free and has a wide range of possible health advantages. Herbal teas are increasingly seen as an integral part of a healthy lifestyle, whether they are used to help digestion, promote relaxation, strengthen the immune system, or support sleep.

The wide variety of flavors and options for personalizing one's tea experience are important factors in the popularity of herbal tea. People can customize their brews to fit their preferences by choosing from a wide variety of herbs and botanicals, whether they prefer calming floral aromas, energizing spices, or refreshing citrus infusions. This variety enables tea enthusiasts to explore and learn new things, developing a distinctive and individualized tea-drinking experience.

Growing online communities and the use of social media have been crucial in raising awareness of herbal tea. Platforms like Instagram,

YouTube, and websites devoted to tea have developed a feeling of community among drinkers, inspiring them to share their experiences, recommendations, and recipes. Herbal tea has become more widely available due to this online presence, which has also created a forum for knowledge sharing and research, further boosting its appeal.

Herbal tea fits in nicely with these principles in a time when environmental awareness and sustainability are at the forefront of consumer concerns. Herbal tea is frequently produced with minimal processing and with ingredients that have been ethically and organically gathered. People who are conscious of their environmental impact and look for things that are advantageous to both their well-being and the earth are drawn to this eco-friendly component.

The appeal of herbal tea is also due to its availability and practicality. Getting a variety of herbal teas is now simpler than ever due to the rise in specialty tea shops, health food stores, and online suppliers. In addition, the availability of tea bags and pre-packaged herbal blends has simplified and made it hassle-free for people with hectic schedules to still enjoy the health advantages of herbal infusions.

There are many reasons why herbal tea is becoming more and more popular, including a resurgence in interest in conventional treatments, a focus on health and wellness, a wide variety of flavors and customization options, the influence of social media, sustainability issues, and the ease in which herbal teas can be obtained. Its popularity is likely to increase as more people become aware of the possible advantages and distinctive sensory experiences that herbal tea may provide. Herbal tea has evolved from a simple beverage to a representation of mindfulness, natural healing, and living a healthy existence.

## Benefits of herbal tea

The enticing flavors of herbal tea, commonly referred to as tisanes, and its potential health advantages have made it extremely popular. Herbal teas have long been valued for their medical qualities and holistic wellness effects in addition to being a soothing and refreshing beverage. In this section, we will examine the several advantages of herbal tea, from physical to mental health, and the scientific research that supports these claims.

Herbal teas are high in antioxidants, which play an important role in neutralizing harmful free radicals in the body. Antioxidants aid in the reduction of oxidative stress, which is linked to aging and a number of chronic diseases. The high antioxidant content of popular herbal teas including chamomile, green tea, and rooibos promotes cellular health and general wellbeing.

Numerous herbal teas have gastrointestinal benefits that help calm the stomach, ease indigestion, and promote overall digestive health. For instance, peppermint tea has long been used to treat bloating, gas, and abdominal discomfort. Ginger tea is popular for its anti-inflammatory qualities and can ease motion and nausea. The appropriate digestion and absorption of nutrients depend on a healthy gut microbiome, which herbal teas can help to support.

Because they promote calmness and relaxation, herbal teas are frequently sought for. With its delicate floral aroma, chamomile tea is recognized for its calming effects on the nervous system as well as its capacity to encourage relaxation and better sleep. Another herbal infusion that helps with anxiety management and better sleep is valerian root tea. Warm herbal tea drinking itself can be a ritual that encourages mindfulness and stress reduction.

Many herbal teas are known for strengthening the immune system. Due to its potential to improve immune response, echinacea tea is a popular choice throughout the cold and flu season. Elderberry tea provides a natural defense against viral infections since it is high in vitamins and antioxidants. Herbal teas' immune-boosting qualities can aid in strengthening the body's built-in defenses and lowering the risk of contracting common illnesses.

Chronic inflammation has been related to a number of diseases, such as arthritis, cancer, and cardiovascular disease. Turmeric and green tea are two herbal drinks that have anti-inflammatory ingredients that can help reduce inflammation in the body. Regular use of these teas may lower your risk of developing chronic inflammatory disorders.

Due to their high water content, herbal teas help meet daily hydration requirements while also having other health advantages. Herbal tea can support healthy hydration levels, supporting all body processes. Additionally, some herbal teas, such as nettle and dandelion, have diuretic effects that aid in natural detoxification by increasing urine production and eliminating toxins from the body.

Some herbal teas have been linked to better metabolism and weight management. For instance, the compounds in green tea can increase metabolism and encourage the burning of fat. Studies on the potential benefits of herbal teas for weight loss and lowering body mass index (BMI), such as oolong and hibiscus tea, have also been conducted.

A number of herbal teas improve cardiovascular health. It has been demonstrated that hibiscus tea, which is distinguished by its vibrant red color, can help lower blood pressure and enhance cholesterol levels. By improving circulation and lessening blood vessel constriction, hawthorn berry tea may enhance heart health. As part of a balanced lifestyle, regular consumption of these herbal teas can help maintain a healthier cardiovascular system.

Herbal teas have a wide range of potential health advantages, including digestive aid, immune support, relaxation, and heart health. They also have antioxidant and anti-inflammatory properties. Though their effectiveness has been supported by centuries of tradition, science is still working to understand the underlying mechanisms and confirm their therapeutic benefits. With each sip offering a holistic boost to both body and mind, incorporating herbal teas into one's daily routine can be a tasty and delightful method to enhance overall well-being.

## Overview of the e-book

An e-book titled "Herbal Tea for Beginners: The Art of Herbal Infusions - Simple Techniques for Making Perfect Herbal Tea" acts as a comprehensive guide for anybody interested in learning more about the world of herbal tea. This e-book seeks to give readers the knowledge and skills they need to make delicious and advantageous herbal infusions. Readers will learn more about herbal tea, its rising popularity, the advantages it provides, and the methods necessary to brew the ideal cup of herbal tea by exploring the outlined chapters.

## Introduction

The e-book begins with an introduction that sums up the significance of herbal tea's expanding appeal. It emphasizes how health-conscious people and tea enthusiasts have begun to favor herbal tea as a beverage. The chapter's introductory section emphasizes the growing popularity of natural and holistic approaches to wellness and lays the groundwork for the remaining chapters.

## Chapter 1: Understanding Herbal Tea

The concept of herbal tea is thoroughly explored in this chapter, along with how it differs from true tea and the different types of herbal tea that are available. The chapter also delves into the possible health advantages of drinking herbal tea, highlighting its appeal beyond its alluring flavors.

## Chapter 2: Getting Started with Herbal Tea

This chapter focuses on the fundamental aspects of making herbal tea to give readers a strong foundation. It offers advice on selecting high-quality herbs, comprehending the required tools and equipment, and effective methods for storing and preserving them. Readers will discover the value of preserving herbs' freshness and learn how to make informed decisions while sourcing herbs.

## Chapter 3: Popular Herbs for Herbal Tea

This chapter explores the world of well-known herbs that are used to make herbal tea. Each herb is examined separately, offering a thorough analysis of its distinctive qualities, tastes, and potential health benefits. Readers can increase their knowledge of herbal teas and experiment with new flavors by reading about herbs including peppermint, chamomile, ginger, lavender, and nettle, among others.

### *Chapter 4: Preparing Herbal Infusions*

In this chapter, the craft of making herbal infusions is highlighted. Readers will discover several infusion methods that are adapted to particular herbs so they can attain the best flavors and health benefits. The part also discusses the technique of blending herbs to create unique flavors and offers advice on water temperature and steeping times. It also provides instructions on how to prepare cooling iced herbal teas for those hot summer days.

### *Chapter 5: Enhancing Your Herbal Tea Experience*

The goal of this chapter is to make drinking herbal tea more enjoyable overall. It explores the technique of adding sweets and flavors to produce distinctive flavor profiles. Furthermore, readers will learn how to match herbal tea with food, revealing complementing flavors and enhancing their culinary experiences. The chapter also discusses the calming and stress-relieving benefits of herbal tea and offers suggestions for picking blends appropriate for various medical conditions.

### *Chapter 6: Exploring Herbal Tea Recipes*

The readers will be exposed to a variety of herbal tea recipes in this chapter. This chapter offers a range of solutions to suit various tastes and needs, from refreshing blends to mood-enhancing infusions and therapeutic treatments. Additionally, there are seasonal recipes that demonstrate the versatility of herbal tea and how it may be enjoyed all year long.

### *Chapter 7: Herbal Tea Etiquette and Culture*

This chapter explores the etiquette and culture related to the consumption of herbal tea in order to provide readers a comprehensive understanding of the beverage. To further enhance their appreciation of this age-old beverage, readers will learn about traditional tea ceremonies, tea rituals from many countries, and even insights on holding their own herbal tea parties.

***Chapter 8: Troubleshooting Common Issues***

This chapter addresses typical problems that could occur while brewing herbal tea. It gives practical solutions for problems including weak or bitter tea, selecting the incorrect herb combinations, and storage and shelf life issues. The chapter also offers advice on how to deal with allergies and sensitivities so that readers can drink herbal tea in safety and comfort.

The e-book comes to a conclusion by summarizing the important ideas covered in each chapter. It highlights the relevance of herbal tea as a healthy, natural beverage and emphasizes its advantages for general wellbeing. The conclusion encourages readers to continue learning about herbal tea and expresses excitement for their upcoming tea journeys and the discoveries that may lie ahead.

"Herbal Tea for Beginners: The Art of Herbal Infusions - Simple Techniques for Making Perfect Herbal Tea" equips readers with the knowledge and skills required to start a flavorful and healthy tea journey by giving a thorough overview of herbal tea, its advantages, and the techniques required to create perfect infusions.

# Chapter I

# Understanding Herbal Tea

## What is herbal tea?

Since ancient times, people from all over the world have sipped on herbal tea, also known as tisane. While the term "tea" is typically used to refer to drinks made from the Camellia sinensis plant, herbal tea deviates from this definition because it is made by fusing a variety of herbs, flowers, spices, and other botanical ingredients. We will dig into the intriguing world of herbal tea in this section, learning about its history, ways of making it, its flavors, and the health advantages it provides.

A beverage known as herbal tea is created by steeping fresh or dried herbs, flowers, fruits, spices, and other plant materials in hot water. Herbal tea does not contain tea leaves, in contrast to true tea, which comes from the Camellia sinensis plant. Instead, it derives its tastes, aromas, and potential health advantages from a wide range of botanical sources, providing a diversified spectrum of flavors and therapeutic characteristics.

Herbal infusions have been consumed for thousands of years and have a profound cultural importance in many communities. Ancient societies, including the Egyptians, Greeks, and Chinese, were aware of the therapeutic benefits of plants and used herbal infusions in their medical procedures. Each culture developed its own distinct herbal traditions as a result of the soothing, energizing, and restorative effects of herbal teas.

There are several ways to make herbal tea, including steeping, decoction, and infusion. During the process of steeping, the herbs are submerged in hot water, and after a predetermined amount of time, the herbs are removed from the water. This process extracts the herbs' flavors as well as their active compounds. On the other hand, decoction involves simmering more difficult plant materials, like roots and bark, in water to extract their essence. The term "infusion" describes the longer-term steeping of herbs in cold water, usually employed with fragile herbs and flowers.

Herbal tea has a wide variety of flavors, which is one of its most appealing qualities. An infinite variety of flavor profiles are available due to the wide variety of herbs, flowers, fruits, and spices. Each herbal infusion offers a distinctive sensory experience, allowing people to delight in a wide range of flavors and fragrances, from calming chamomile and energizing peppermint to spicy ginger and fragrant lavender.

Herbal tea is well known for its medicinal and potential health qualities. Different herbs have particular therapeutic properties that can promote overall health. For instance, chamomile tea is well known for its relaxing effects, which promote rest and sleep. Ginger tea may aid with nausea and inflammation, while peppermint tea can ease gastrointestinal pain. Herbal tea is a popular choice for those looking for natural remedies and holistic approaches to wellbeing because each plant has a unique set of potential health benefits.

Herbal tea's lack of caffeine is one of its noticeable qualities. Herbal infusions offer a caffeine-free alternative for anyone looking for a beverage that won't disturb sleep patterns or create caffeine-related negative effects, unlike true tea, which naturally includes caffeine. Because of this, herbal tea is a good option for those who are sensitive to caffeine, women who are pregnant, and those who want to cut back on their caffeine intake.

The versatility of herbal tea extends well beyond the realm of simple infusions of a single ingredient. Herbal tea blends, which are expertly formulated mixtures of various herbs and botanicals, provide a fun method to create distinctive and customized flavors. Individuals can customize their tea experience by blending herbs, resulting in a harmony of flavors and therapeutic effects. The practice of blending herbal teas encourages exploration and motivates people to discover and develop their own blends.

Beyond its health advantages, herbal tea has a unique place in the worlds of ritual, self-care, and relaxation. Herbal tea preparation and consumption can be a thoughtful practice that fosters peace and well-being. Herbal tea fosters periods of introspection and tranquility in the midst of busy lives, whether it is consumed alone or with others.

The flavors and medicinal benefits of numerous herbs, flowers, fruits, and spices are combined to create the enticing beverage known as herbal tea. Herbal tea gives tea enthusiasts and those looking for natural remedies an alluring and holistic experience due to its deep historical roots, wide variety of flavors, and potential health advantages. Herbal tea continues to enchant and motivate tea enthusiasts all over the world, whether for rest and relaxation, renewal, or simply the joy of sipping a warm cup of fragrant infusion.

## Differentiating herbal tea from true tea

Tea is a beloved beverage with a long history and cultural significance that is enjoyed worldwide. It is crucial to distinguish between true tea and herbal tea, commonly referred to as tisane, while talking about tea. While both offer a beautiful and cozy sipping experience, there are considerable differences in their ingredients and production techniques. In this section, we'll look into the qualities that set herbal tea apart from true tea and examine each beverage's history, plant sources, methods of production, flavors, and health advantages.

The leaves of the East Asian native Camellia sinensis plant are used to make true tea. Tea of all varieties, including green, black, oolong, and white, are produced by this plant species. Variations in cultivation, processing, and oxidation levels are the cause of these teas' differences. Caffeine, a substance that is naturally present in tea leaves, is found in the Camellia sinensis plant.

The Camellia sinensis plant is not the source of herbal tea, often known as tisane. Instead, it is made by steeping a variety of herbs, including flowers, fruits, spices, and other botanical ingredients, in hot water. Herbal tea is naturally caffeine-free and does not contain tea leaves. Herbal tea infusions have a wide range of flavors, fragrances, and potential health benefits due to the extensive diversity of botanicals employed.

The origins of true tea can be found in both ancient Chinese and Indian cultures. Tea was grown and consumed throughout Asia before eventually making its way to Europe and other parts of the world. Tea rituals and ceremonies have developed into important aspects of many cultures. Contrarily, herbal tea has its roots in several parts of the world, with each culture embracing native herbs and botanicals for their culinary and medicinal qualities.

Only the Camellia sinensis plant produces true tea. However, the features of the finished product are influenced by things like the soil, climate, and processing methods. True tea is produced in a number of distinct forms by the Camellia sinensis plant, depending on the variety. Herbal tea, on the other hand, derives its flavors and medicinal qualities from a wide variety of botanical sources, including fruits like berries and citrus, flowers like hibiscus and lavender, spices like ginger and cinnamon, and herbs like chamomile and mint.

True tea is processed through rolling, oxidation, drying, and withering. Depending on the kind of tea you want, these stages vary. For instance, black tea completely oxidizes while green tea only partially does so. Between these two extremes is oolong tea. Herbal tea, on the other hand, is often made by simply steeping botanical materials in hot water without the need of any other processing methods besides drying or dehydration.

True tea comes in a variety of flavors and aromas depending on the type of tea, the growing environment, and the processing. Green tea frequently has flavors that are grassy, vegetal, or nutty. Black tea typically has malty or earthy undertones and is strong. Oolong tea comes in a wide range of flavors, from fruity and fragrant to toasted and complex. Herbal tea, on the other hand, offers a wide variety of flavors depending on the botanicals utilized. While peppermint tea has a cooling, minty flavor, chamomile tea has a floral, almost apple-like flavor.

Since green tea, black tea, and white tea contain catechins, antioxidants, and other bioactive compounds, these teas are known for their potential health benefits. These teas have been studied for their potential benefits on immunological support, weight management, heart health, and cognitive function. With its wide variety of botanical compounds, herbal tea also has a number of potential health advantages. For instance, ginger tea may help with digestion and reduce inflammation, while chamomile tea is well recognized for its calming effects.

The presence of caffeine is a key distinction between true tea and herbal tea. Except for herbal infusions made from Camellia sinensis leaves, true tea contains caffeine. The amount of caffeine that can be found in true tea varies depending on a number of factors including the type of tea and how it is brewed. Herbal tea, on the other hand, is naturally caffeine-free, making it a fantastic option for people who are sensitive to it or desire to avoid it for a variety of reasons.

For tea enthusiasts, as well as those looking for particular flavor profiles or health advantages, understanding the distinction between true tea and herbal tea is crucial. While herbal tea includes a wide range of botanical infusions that are naturally caffeine-free, true tea comes from the Camellia sinensis plant and contains caffeine. True tea and herbal tea both have distinctive flavors, aromas, and potential health advantages, expanding the world's tea culture and giving people a wide range of options that suit their tastes and wellness objectives.

## Varieties of herbal tea

The alluring beverage herbal tea, sometimes referred to as tisane, has a wide variety of flavors, aromas, and potential health advantages. Herbal tea is made by steeping a variety of herbs, flowers, fruits, spices, and other botanical ingredients in hot water, as opposed to true tea, which comes from the Camellia sinensis plant. In this section, we'll take a wonderful tour of the different herbal tea variations while examining the unique qualities and advantages of well-known herbs, unique blends, and regional specialties.

The dried flowers of the chamomile plant are used to make the relaxing and calming beverage known as chamomile tea. It has a delicate flavor that is flowery with a hint of sweetness that is apple-like. Before going to bed, many people drink chamomile tea to help them unwind, fall asleep, and reduce stress and anxiety.

The flavor characteristic of peppermint tea, which is prepared from the plant's leaves, is energizing and refreshing. Because peppermint leaves contain menthol, which has a cooling effect, they are frequently used to relieve headaches, promote respiratory health, and ease digestive discomfort. Additionally favored for its boosting and invigorating qualities is peppermint tea.

The flavor of ginger tea, which is made from the plant's roots, is warm, spicy, and just a little bit sweet. It is well known for its potential digestive advantages, which may lessen bloating, indigestion, and nausea. Ginger tea is a well-liked option for easing muscular discomfort and lowering bodily inflammation because it also has anti-inflammatory effects.

Hibiscus tea has an acidic, tangy flavor with a hint of natural sweetness and is prepared from the vibrant calyces of the hibiscus flower. This antioxidant-rich, ruby-colored infusion has a number of health advantages, including supporting heart health, helping to regulate blood pressure, and having immune-stimulating effects.

The rooibos plant's leaves are used to make the South African beverage Rooibos tea. It has an organically sweet and earthy flavor that is frequently characterized as nutty or woody. Due to its lack of caffeine and abundance in antioxidants, Rooibos tea is a preferred beverage for unwinding, developing healthy skin, and enhancing overall well-being.

The fragrant purple blossoms of the lavender plant are used to make lavender tea, which has a delicate, floral scent. It has a mild, calming flavor that is frequently savored to lower stress levels, encourage relaxation, and enhance the quality of sleep. You can drink lavender tea on its own or combine it with other herbs for a calming infusion.

The flavor of lemon balm tea, which is produced from the plant's leaves, is lemony and citrusy with a hint of sweetness. This herb is well-liked for lowering anxiety, enhancing cognitive function, and fostering a sense of well-being because it is frequently linked to relaxation and mood enhancement.

The stinging nettle plant's leaves are used to make nettle tea, which has a distinctive earthy and grassy flavor. The benefits of nettle tea include potential cleansing effects, support for a healthy digestive system, and enhancement of overall well-being. Additionally, it has a lot of nutrients like calcium, iron, and vitamins A and C.

Herbal tea blends offer a delightful fusion of flavors and advantages in addition to the benefits of individual herbs. To generate rich and pleasing flavor profiles, these blends frequently incorporate complementing herbs, flowers, fruits, and spices. For instance, chamomile, lavender, and lemon balm can be combined to make a calming and scented infusion that encourages rest and sleep.

Different parts of the world each have their own distinctive herbal tea specialties. As an illustration, Indian Ayurvedic herbal teas blend Ayurvedic herbs and spices to produce blends that are designed to assist particular health needs and encourage balance. Moroccan mint tea, made with green tea and fresh mint leaves, is a staple in Moroccan culture and a representation of hospitality. The world of herbal tea is made more diverse and richly cultural by the indigenous herbs and traditional tea preparations from each place.

A plethora of flavors, aromas, and potential health advantages can be found in the many herbal tea variations. Each herbal tea offers a different sensory experience, from the calming chamomile and energizing peppermint to the tangy hibiscus and earthy rooibos. Herbal tea continues to delight tea enthusiasts all over the world with its broad variety of alternatives, whether it is consumed for relaxation, digestion, immune support, or simply the enjoyment of a tasty cup. Discover the potential health advantages of nature's botanical wonders as you travel through the different herbal tea varieties, savoring the rich tapestry of flavors.

## Health benefits of herbal tea

The potential health advantages of herbal tea, commonly referred to as tisane, have long been applauded. This delightful beverage gives more than simply a flavorful and relaxing experience because it is made from a wide variety of herbs, flowers, fruits, and spices. This section will examine the numerous health advantages of drinking herbal tea while highlighting the distinctive qualities of individual herbs and their possible advantages for different aspects of wellbeing.

Antioxidants, which aid in defending the body against the harmful effects of free radicals, are present in abundance in many herbal teas. Free radicals have been associated with a number of diseases and can lead to oxidative stress. Herbs with a high antioxidant content, such rooibos, hibiscus, and green tea, are good for your overall health.

The digestive properties of certain plants used in herbal tea blends are well known. For instance, peppermint tea has long been used to treat indigestion, bloating, and other stomach discomforts. Due to its inherent anti-inflammatory properties, ginger tea can help soothe the digestive system and lessen motion sickness. Chamomile tea is a popular choice for reducing digestive disturbances because of its well-known ability for having a mild calming effect on the stomach.

Numerous herbal teas have calming and stress-relieving effects that help people feel calm and well-being. With its moderate sedative properties, chamomile tea is frequently used before bed to encourage relaxation and enhance the quality of sleep. The calming scent of lavender tea is well known, and it can help people feel less stressed and anxious. It has been demonstrated that lemon balm tea improves mood and cognitive performance, reducing stress and fostering calm.

Some herbal teas are well known for strengthening the immune system and assisting the body's defense mechanisms. The immune system is said to be strengthened by echinacea tea, which also shortens the duration and intensity of cold and flu symptoms. Elderberry tea, which is high in vitamins and antioxidants, is well known for its ability to boost immunity and protect against respiratory infections.

Many chronic diseases are triggered by inflammation, and herbal teas can help reduce inflammation in the body. Curcumin, a potent anti-inflammatory compound found in turmeric, has drawn attention for its ability to treat arthritic symptoms, improve joint health, and lower inflammatory levels in the body. In addition to its anti-inflammatory qualities, ginger tea may offer relief for ailments including osteoarthritis.

Heart-healthy benefits have been associated with a number of herbal teas. Hibiscus tea has been proven to decrease blood pressure and enhance cholesterol levels due to its vibrant hue and tangy flavor. Green tea, which is high in antioxidants and catechins, has the potential to support cardiovascular health by lowering the risk of heart disease and enhancing blood lipid profiles.

Herbal teas can be a useful addition to a weight-loss plan. Studies on green tea's potential to increase metabolism and support weight loss have been conducted. With its inherent ability to decrease appetite, peppermint tea can assist in reducing cravings and fostering satiety. Dandelion tea helps with cleansing and water weight loss because of its diuretic qualities.

Some herbal teas have been shown to improve cognitive function, mental clarity, and focus. Ginseng tea, which is made from the ginseng plant, has long been used to boost mental acuity, memory, and focus. With its invigorating scent, rosemary tea is thought to improve cognitive function and may even be neuroprotective.

Herbal tea has potential health advantages in addition to being a delectable and soothing beverage. The world of herbal tea offers a wide range of health-promoting options, from the antioxidant qualities of green tea to the calming effects of chamomile and the immune-boosting properties of echinacea. Herbal tea, which offers a sip of nature's infused elixir, can give a natural and delightful way to support overall well-being as part of a balanced lifestyle.

# Chapter II

# Getting Started with Herbal Tea

**Selecting high-quality herbs**

The selection of high-quality herbs is the first step on the journey to a remarkable cup of herbal tea. The quality of the herbs used in herbal tea is essential to creating a superior and gratifying brew, just as the flavor and health benefits of a dish are influenced by the quality of the ingredients. The crucial elements to think about while selecting herbs for herbal tea, such as sourcing, freshness, appearance, aroma, and storage procedures, will be covered in this section. You may take your herbal tea experience to new heights by nourishing your senses and selecting high-quality herbs.

Thinking about the source of your herbs is the first step in selecting high-quality ones. Seek out reputable suppliers who have an emphasis on sustainability and quality. A purer and more natural product is provided by organic certification, which guarantees that the herbs are grown without the use of synthetic pesticides, herbicides, or fertilizers. It is also worthwhile to look into regional herbalists, farmers' markets, or internet resources that focus on high-quality herbs purchased directly from reliable growers.

Herb quality is largely influenced by how recently they were harvested. Herbs keep their original hues, flavors, and fragrances when properly collected, dried, and preserved. Select herbs that have recently been harvested since they are more likely to be vibrant and abundant in essential oils. A deterioration in quality is indicated by herbs that appear dull, faded, or have lost their distinctive aroma.

Herbs' aesthetic attractiveness might reveal valuable information about their quality. Look at the herbs' appearance, taking note of their color, texture, and overall condition. Fresh and strong plants usually have stunning hues, such deep green or vibrant purple. The leaves or flowers must be undamaged, unblemished, and free from any traces of mold or pests. Herbs of high-quality have a distinctly vibrant and welcoming appearance.

Herbs' scent is a delightful indicator of the flavors and advantages they will impart to your tea. To release the aroma of the herbs, lightly crush or rub them between your fingers. The essential oils and active ingredients in high-quality herbs will give off a potent and distinctive smell. Whether it's the calming notes of chamomile or the energizing scent of peppermint, each herb has its own distinctive aroma. The aroma should be enticing, fresh, and devoid of any unpleasant or musty odors.

Herbs must be stored properly to retain their potency and quality over time. Herbs should be kept out of direct sunlight, moisture, and heat while being stored in sealed containers. These elements can cause the herbs to lose flavor, aroma, and healthy ingredients as a result of exposure. Select herbs that are sealed in bags or containers that offer the best defense against environmental elements. Furthermore, make sure to keep your herbs dry and cool, ideally in a dark pantry or cupboard.

Various herbs use different plant parts, such as leaves, flowers, stems, roots, or a combination of these. Knowing which plant parts are utilized to make herbal tea will help you understand its flavor and potential health advantages. For instance, chamomile tea is made from the flowers, which have calming effects, whereas ginger tea gets its spice and digestive advantages from the root. To align with your desired flavor profile and health objectives, take into account the precise plant parts used in herbal tea blends.

When in doubt or trying out new herbal teas, look for feedback as well as recommendations from reliable sources. Based on their experiences with various herb suppliers and tea blends, online platforms, herbalist websites, tea groups, and other tea enthusiasts can provide insightful advice. Take into account their advice and knowledge to improve your process of choosing high-quality herbs.

A high-quality herbal tea experience begins with the sensory and thoughtful process of selecting high-quality ingredients. You can make sure the herbs you use for your brew are of the greatest quality by choosing reliable sources, emphasizing freshness, appreciating appearance and aroma, putting correct storage methods into place, and taking into account the components used in herbal tea blends. You can enjoy the vibrant flavors, wonderful aromas, and potential health advantages that herbal tea has to offer by nourishing your senses and selecting high-quality herbs. This will make your tea rituals more enjoyable.

## Tools and equipment for making herbal tea

The selection of herbs and flavors is only one aspect of the skill of creating herbal tea. In order to improve the brewing process and extract the herbs' full flavor, it also entails the use of appropriate tools and equipment. We will explore necessary items like tea infusers, teapots, kettles, strainers, and temperature control devices as we delve into the world of tools and equipment for making herbal tea in this section. You can advance your herbal tea journey and produce a perfect brew each and every time by understanding the function and advantages of these tools.

Herbal tea brewing requires the use of a tea infuser. These tools keep the herbs confined for simple removal while allowing them to soak in hot water. Tea infusers come in a variety of shapes and sizes, including mesh, ball, and basket infusers. Select an infuser that allows for optimum water circulation and is appropriate for the size of the herbs you plan to utilize. Tea infusers can be made of a variety of materials, including silicone, stainless steel, or mesh, each of which has benefits in terms of heat conductivity, durability, and ease of cleaning.

Teapots are vessels that make steeping and pouring herbal tea easier and are both useful and visually beautiful. Pick a teapot made of heat-resistant components like glass, ceramic, or cast iron. Teapots made of ceramic and cast iron retain heat very well, while glass teapots let you see the brewing process. Pick a teapot with an integrated infuser or an additional infuser basket to make the steeping procedure simple and clean.

An electric kettle is a useful addition to your collection of herbal teas because it offers ease and accuracy while boiling water. To guarantee that you can heat water to the ideal temperature for each herb or tea blend, look for an electric kettle with adjustable temperature settings. For the best flavor and medicinal ingredient extraction, different plants need different water temperatures. You can obtain the desired temperature range with electric kettles that have temperature control options, whether you want a gentle simmer for delicate herbs or a rolling boil for strong infusions.

For filtering herbal tea and getting rid of any residue or sediment, strainers are necessary. To make a smooth and satisfying cup of tea, drain the infused liquid after the herbs have steeped in the teapot or cup. To properly catch any stray particles, choose a strainer with a fine mesh or tiny holes. There is no need for an additional straining apparatus because some teapots include built-in strainers.

It's essential to maintain the proper temperature during the brewing process to extract the tastes and healthy ingredients from the herbs. The water temperature is precisely tracked by temperature control equipment like thermometers and smart kettles. You can use these instruments to follow particular temperature recommendations for various herbs, guaranteeing that you always get the best brew. The therapeutic properties and flavor profile of your herbal tea can both be improved by making an investment in a dependable temperature control equipment.

Although it isn't technically an equipment for preparing tea, the choice of mugs or cups might influence how tea is consumed. Choose mugs or cups made of heat-resistant materials that keep their warmth, like double-walled glass or ceramic. Additionally, pick a size and shape that enables relaxed sipping and scent pleasure. Some cups include built-in lids or strainers, making it simple to steep tea right in the cup and keep it hot for longer periods of time.

Herbs must be stored properly to keep their potency and freshness. To maintain the quality of your herbal tea ingredients, invest on airtight jars or containers. These containers ought to be created from opaque materials that keep out light and moisture, such metal or glass. To ensure proper rotation and use of the herbs, label the containers with the name of the plant and the date of harvest. Herbs retain their flavors, aromas, and health benefits when stored properly, resulting in consistently high-quality tea.

A great brewing experience is greatly influenced by the instruments and equipment used to prepare herbal tea. A perfect brew can be made with the use of a variety of tools, including tea infusers, teapots, temperature-controlled electric kettles, strainers, and storage containers. You can improve the flavors, aromas, and therapeutic qualities of your herbal tea by choosing high-quality tools and equipment that suit your preferences. Accept the craft of making tea, and relish in the voyage as you explore the beautiful world of herbal infusions.

## Proper storage and preservation of herbs

Herbs are priceless gifts from nature because of their alluring scents, eye-catching colors, and healing qualities. It is essential to store and preserve herbs properly if you want to completely appreciate their flavors and take advantage of their health advantages. In this section, we'll cover the significance of preserving herbs properly by exploring things like light, moisture, temperature, containers, and labeling. You can increase the shelf life, maintain the strength, and guarantee a satisfying and pleasant herbal experience by knowing how to preserve herbs correctly.

Herbs that are exposed to light may lose some of their flavor, aroma, and medicinal components. Herbs should be kept in opaque jars or containers to prevent exposure to light. Avoid containers that are clear or translucent and enable light to pass through. Additionally, pick a storage area out of the path of direct sunlight, like a dim pantry or cabinet. Herbs' freshness and fragrant and therapeutic qualities can be preserved by protecting them from light.

Storage of herbs is frequently harmed by moisture. The quality and security of the herbs may be at risk due to bacteria, mold, or mildew growth brought on by excessive moisture. Before storing herbs, make sure they are totally dry to avoid moisture buildup. Consider using a dehydrator or continuing to air-dry herbs if they are just a little damp to get rid of any remaining moisture. Additionally, choose storage containers with an airtight cover to prevent moisture from penetrating. To remove excess moisture and preserve the integrity of the herbs, silica gel packets can also be put to herb containers.

The preservation of the flavors, fragrances, and therapeutic components in herbs depends heavily on temperature. Herbs should typically be kept dry, cool, and at a somewhat constant temperature. Condensation and rotting can result from extreme temperature fluctuations. Herbs shouldn't be kept close to heat sources like stoves or ovens since heat might degrade their strength. Depending on the particular herb, the recommended storage temperature ranges from 50°F to 70°F (10°C to 21°C). While other herbs may maintain their quality at room temperature, some delicate herbs may benefit from refrigeration to keep them fresh.

To preserve the freshness and potency of herbs, the correct storage containers must be used. Choose airtight containers, such as glass jars with screw-top lids or metal tins with snug-fitting coverings, that are composed of materials that are impermeable to air and moisture. These containers prevent oxidation and keep the therapeutic benefits, flavor, and essential oils of the plants. Plastic containers should not be used since they might not offer enough protection and can absorb odors. In order to reduce air exposure and maximize the preservation of the herbs' properties, choose containers that are the right size.

It's essential to label your herb containers for optimal rotation and identification. Each container should be clearly marked with the name of the herb and the date of harvest or purchase. You may monitor the freshness of your herbs using this information and make sure that older herbs are consumed before newer ones. The source of the herbs should also be mentioned for future reference and repurchasing. Using labels will keep you organized, ensure that your herb supply is always fresh, and increase the effectiveness and enjoyment of your herbal concoctions.

Several factors determine whether to keep herbs as entire leaves or as pulverized powder. Compared to powdered herbs, whole leaves typically keep their flavor and potency longer. To preserve their volatile oils and potent flavors, herbs should ideally be ground soon before use. To preserve the freshness of your herbs, store them in sealed containers away from light and moisture if you prefer the convenience of pre-ground herbs. Regardless of the form, it is crucial to regularly check the herbs' aroma, color, and potency to preserve their freshness and make any adjustments.

Herbs can also be preserved by freezing and drying in addition to traditional preservation methods. Herbs can keep more of their aromas and flavors by being frozen. The herbs should be carefully cleaned and dried before being put in labeled freezer bags or ice cube trays with some water or oil. You may use herbs conveniently all year round with this strategy. Herbs can be preserved longer by being dried, either naturally or with the aid of a dehydrator. Herbs that have been properly dried can be kept in sealed containers and utilized in cooking or as a medicine.

Herbs must be stored and preserved properly in order to maintain their medicinal properties, tastes, and freshness. You can increase the shelf life of your herbs and benefit from them for a longer period of time by shielding them from light, moisture, and extreme temperatures, selecting appropriate containers, labeling for identification and rotation, and taking alternative preservation techniques like freezing or drying into consideration. Your culinary and wellness experiences will be enhanced if you treat your herbs with care and respect. They will reward you with their alluring scents, brilliant colors, and potent essences.

## Understanding herbal tea labels

Understanding the information provided on tea labels is essential while exploring the world of herbal tea in order to choose the ideal blend and make informed decisions. Labels for herbal tea include valuable information about the blend's components, history, certifications, and brewing directions. We will examine the key elements of herbal tea labels in this section, arming you with the knowledge you need to correctly interpret and assess the information being provided. You may confidently navigate the large selection of possibilities and find teas that suit your preferences and values by studying herbal tea labels.

An extensive list of the plants used in the blend is provided in the ingredients section of a herbal tea label. It enables you to recognize the primary and secondary herbs, spices, flowers, fruits, or other organic components that contribute to flavor and aroma. To have a better sense of the tea's potential flavor profile, become familiar with popular herbal ingredients and their qualities. To make sure the tea complies with your dietary needs, pay close attention to any potential allergies or additives indicated in the ingredient list.

Herbal tea packages with organic or certified labels have been produced in accordance with strict cultivation, processing, and sourcing guidelines. With organic certification, you may be guaranteed that no synthetic pesticides, herbicides, or genetically modified organisms (GMOs) were used in the tea's growth. Look for certifications from recognized organizations that are equal to the USDA Organic, EU Organic, or equivalent certifications. With the help of these certifications, tea can be produced in a way that promotes environmental sustainability and limits exposure to hazardous chemicals.

The origin country can tell you a lot about how and where the herbal tea was produced. The flavor, aroma, and quality of the herbs can vary depending on the place due to the varied soil types and temperature patterns. You can discover teas from locations acknowledged for generating great herbal types by learning about the country of origin. For instance, rooibos from South Africa, peppermint from the United States, or chamomile from Egypt. Exploring teas from various origins might result in fascinating discoveries and distinctive flavor encounters.

The harvest date, which is not typically included on herbal tea labels, offers information on the tea's potency and freshness. Some tea manufacturers take pride in stating the precise year or season in which the herbs were harvested. Fresher herbs typically have more brilliant aromas and higher concentrations of essential oils, making tea sipping more enjoyable. Select teas with recent or particular harvest dates since they tend to have herbs that are of higher quality and offer the best flavors and smells.

The ideal steeping time, water temperature, and proportions to achieve the greatest flavor and aroma are provided in the brewing directions on herbal tea labels. For any herb to perform to its best capacity, specific brewing conditions are needed. Pay close attention to the recommended temperature range because some delicate herbs may need lower temperatures to maintain their delicate flavors. As a starting point, adhere to the directions, then make adjustments based on your individual taste preferences. You can discover special qualities of several herbal teas by experimenting with brewing parameters.

To warn customers to potential allergies present in the tea, tea labels may include allergen warnings. Nuts, soy, gluten, and other ingredients that potentially provoke negative responses in sensitive people are common allergens that may be indicated. To make sure the tea is safe to consume if you have any known allergies or dietary restrictions, carefully read the allergen warnings. If you have specific questions, it's typically good to speak with the tea company or contact their customer care.

Some herbal tea labels disclose the company's commitment to social responsibility, fair trade, or sustainability. Look for certifications that emphasize the brand's commitment to ethical sourcing, fair compensation for farmers, and environmental preservation, such as Fair Trade Certified, Rainforest Alliance, or comparable indicators. You can help make the tea business more equitable and sustainable by supporting companies who place a high priority on sustainability and ethical behavior.

Understanding the information on the labels of herbal teas gives you the power to choose products that suit your tastes, values, and dietary requirements. You can start a tea journey that is both joyful and mindful by understanding the information offered on labels, such as ingredients, organic certifications, country of origin, harvest dates, brewing instructions, allergen warnings, and sustainability practices. Let the labels serve as your guide as you discover the many varieties of herbal teas and enjoy their distinct flavors, aromas, and health advantages.

# Chapter III

## Popular Herbs for Herbal Tea

### Peppermint

With its energizing aroma and cooling flavor, peppermint has long been cherished as a well-liked herb for herbal tea. Peppermint tea has grown significantly in popularity among tea enthusiasts all over the world due to its soothing and cooling qualities. We will explore the history, characteristics, health advantages, and several applications of peppermint in herbal tea in this section. Peppermint continues to fascinate our senses and provide a delightful tea-drinking experience because of its long history and therapeutic benefits.

Mentha piperita, or peppermint, is a hybrid mint plant that originated from the cross-breeding of spearmint (Mentha spicata) and water mint (Mentha aquatica). For its therapeutic and culinary benefits, it has been grown and used for centuries. The Egyptians, Greeks, and Romans were among the early civilizations who used peppermint as a natural remedy. Peppermint tea is still a popular herbal infusion that people drink nowadays all around the world.

Its lively and energizing flavor profile is one of peppermint tea's distinguishing features. Menthol, which gives peppermint plants their cooling effect and distinctive mint flavor, can be found in their leaves. The leaves release their essential oils when steeped in hot water, creating a refreshing and fragrant tea. For those looking for an energizing and uplifting beverage, peppermint tea is a popular option due to its strong, minty flavor with a hint of sweetness.

Numerous health advantages of peppermint tea have increased its appeal as a herbal infusion. Supporting digestive health is one of its best-known advantages. Traditional remedies for indigestion, bloating, and stomach discomfort include peppermint. Smooth digestion is encouraged by the menthol in peppermint, which helps to calm gastrointestinal system muscles. Additionally, it's thought that peppermint tea has antimicrobial and antioxidant characteristics that boost immune system health and general wellbeing.

Beyond its flavor, peppermint tea also has fragrant qualities. It has been demonstrated that the aroma of peppermint has calming and soothing effects on the body and mind. A cup of peppermint tea can aid with stress relief, relaxation, and tension headache relief. The natural muscle relaxant properties of menthol found in peppermint help to gently relieve muscular aches and pains. It can be calming and energizing to include peppermint tea in your self-care routine.

In addition to being used in tea, peppermint is a multipurpose herb. To add a blast of minty taste to salads, desserts, and cocktails, use the fresh leaves as a garnish. It is common practice to utilize peppermint oil or extract in aromatherapy, confectionary, and baking goods. Additionally, peppermint can be used to make distinctive tea blends like peppermint-chamomile or peppermint-lavender by combining it with other herbs and botanicals. Peppermint is a great choice for both culinary and wellness uses because of its versatility.

While most people can safely drink peppermint tea, there are a few things to bear in mind. Due to its potential to relax the lower esophageal sphincter and worsen symptoms, peppermint tea may not be recommended for people with gastroesophageal reflux disease (GERD) or acid reflux. Additionally, people who have menthol or mint sensitivities should use caution when drinking peppermint tea. Before introducing peppermint tea into your regimen, it is always advisable to speak with a healthcare provider if you have any underlying health conditions or concerns.

One of the most beloved and well-liked plants for herbal tea is peppermint. Peppermint tea continues to enthrall tea enthusiasts all over the world with its energizing flavor, cooling scent, and multiple health advantages. Peppermint tea delivers a delightful and revitalizing tea-drinking experience, whether appreciated for its digestive assistance, stress-relieving effects, or simply for its delightful taste. Take in the essence of refreshment and enjoy peppermint tea's calming effects as it stimulates your senses and improves your overall well-being.

## Chamomile

Chamomile has a well-deserved reputation as one of the most widely used plants for herbal tea because of its delicate appearance and calming effects. Chamomile tea has been enjoyed for ages as a soothing and therapeutic beverage due to its calming properties and floral aroma. We will look at the history, characteristics, health advantages, and various applications of chamomile in herbal tea in this section. Chamomile has a long history and is still quite popular today, captivating tea enthusiasts all over the world.

Matricaria chamomilla or Chamaemelum nobile are the scientific names for chamomile, a flowering plant of the daisy family. Its use dates back to the time of the Egyptians, Greeks, and Romans, among other ancient civilizations. The word "chamomile" comes from the Greek words "khamai," which means "on the ground," and "melon," which means "apple," alluding to the plant's low growth and apple-like aroma. One of the oldest and most useful herbs in traditional medicine, chamomile has long been recognized for its healing abilities.

Every sip of chamomile tea delivers a sensation of calm because of its delicate and flowery flavor profile, which is well known. The chamomile plant's blossoms contain essential oils that give the tea a light sweetness and a calming herbal flavor. The scent of fresh flowers and apples is released when chamomile tea is made, producing a calm and welcoming atmosphere. Chamomile tea is a preferred beverage for unwinding and relaxing due to its delicate flavor and nice aroma.

For its soothing effects and capacity to encourage relaxation and sound sleep, chamomile tea is recognized. Compounds in the tea include chamazulene, apigenin, and bisabolol have mild sedative properties and reduce stress and anxiety. Drinking chamomile tea can promote calmness, ease tension, and enhance general wellbeing. It is frequently savored just before bed to induce a restful night's sleep and to foster serenity.

The long-standing reputation of chamomile tea as a digestive aid and pain reliever is well-deserved. Intestinal distress, bloating, and indigestion symptoms can all be relieved with the tea. Chamomile is a soothing and all-natural treatment for digestive problems because of its anti-inflammatory characteristics and capacity to relax smooth muscles. Drinking chamomile tea frequently can help maintain a healthy stomach and promote digestion.

Chamomile has significant advantages for both oral and skin health. To ease skin irritations, promote wound healing, and reduce inflammation, it is frequently used in topical applications including creams, lotions, and ointments. Eczema, psoriasis, and acne are just a few of the skin diseases that can be relieved by chamomile's anti-inflammatory and antibacterial characteristics. In addition, chamomile tea can be used as a mouthwash to reduce gum inflammation, treat oral ulcers, and freshen breath.

Chamomile is used in a variety of dishes in addition to being a herbal tea. The flowers can be used to impart a subtle floral flavor to beverages, baked products, and desserts. Chamomile can be used in ice cream, sorbet, syrup, and even cocktail recipes to provide a sense of flowery richness and elevate the flavors. The versatility of chamomile permits inventive culinary experimentation and gives conventional recipes a unique twist.

Despite the fact that chamomile is typically regarded as being harmless, it is still vital to use caution, especially for people who have known sensitivities to ragweed or other members of the daisy family. Chamomile allergy symptoms can include breathing issues, skin rashes, and itching. Additionally, because chamomile tea may have uterine-stimulating effects, pregnant women should consult with their healthcare professionals before ingesting it.

Tea enthusiasts are captivated by chamomile's gentle flavor, comforting aroma, and curative qualities, which make it a much-loved herb for the preparation of herbal tea. Chamomile has been valued for its relaxing properties, digestive assistance, skin advantages, and culinary versatility from its ancient origins to its current popularity. Chamomile tea provides a wonderful and tranquil tea-drinking experience, whether you're looking for a moment of relaxation, digestive relief, or a fragrant infusion to elevate culinary creations. Explore the many applications of chamomile tea while basking in its curative embrace and embracing the calm that comes with the time-honored tradition of drinking it.

**Ginger**

With its unique flavor and therapeutic benefits, ginger has a well-deserved reputation as one of the most widely used plants in herbal

tea. Ginger tea has been used as a warming and restorative beverage for ages and is well-known for its spicy kick and energizing aroma. We will look at the history, characteristics, health advantages, and various applications of ginger in herbal tea in this section Since it has such a long history and so many medicinal qualities, ginger has captured the attention of tea enthusiasts all around the world.

The flowering plant known as ginger, or Zingiber officinale, is indigenous to Southeast Asia. It has a long history of use in both cooking and traditional medicine. For its therapeutic qualities and unique flavor, ginger was highly valued in ancient civilizations such as China, India, and the Middle East. Ginger plant roots are harvested, dried, and used in a variety of ways, such as fresh ginger, ground ginger, and ginger tea.

Ginger tea is famous for having a potent, robust, and spicy flavor profile. Gingerol, a compound that gives ginger its distinctive flavor and aroma, is found in the plant's root. Ginger's essential oils are released when it is steeped in hot water, creating a comforting and flavorful beverage. Ginger tea is a well-liked option for people looking for an energizing and tasty beverage due to its distinctive blend of spiciness, sweetness, and earthiness.

The potential of ginger to enhance digestive health is one of its most well-known advantages. Ginger has long been used to treat digestive discomfort, bloating, and nausea. Ginger's active ingredients, including gingerol and zingiberene, have anti-inflammatory qualities that can help lessen stomach irritation and facilitate easier digestion.

After meals or when experiencing stomach discomfort, sipping ginger tea can offer relief and enhance overall digestive health.

Due to the significant amount of antioxidants found in ginger, it is known for its ability to strengthen the immune system. Antioxidants aid in the body's defense against oxidative stress and free radicals, which can harm cells and have a role in a number of health issues. Regular ginger tea consumption may improve overall health by boosting the body's defenses, the immune system, and other defenses. The potent antioxidants found in ginger also contribute to its anti-aging benefits and possible advantages for skin health.

Powerful anti-inflammatory properties found in ginger can aid the body by reducing inflammation and easing pain. It has been used for centuries to treat menstrual cramps, stiff joints, and muscle soreness. It can be helpful to recover from exercise-induced muscle damage or inflammatory conditions by drinking ginger tea or using ginger as a compress topically.

Ginger tea is frequently used to ease respiratory disease symptoms like coughing, congestion, and sore throats. Ginger's warming qualities helps ease sore throat tissues, remove congestion, and facilitate easier breathing. The antibacterial and antiviral qualities of ginger tea may also contribute to its potential advantages in promoting respiratory health and avoiding respiratory infections.

The versatility of ginger goes beyond its use in herbal teas. It is a common component in many different cuisines and gives savory and sweet meals a zesty, aromatic touch. While ground ginger gives spice blends, curry powders, and gingerbread their characteristic flavor, fresh ginger can be used in stir-fries, soups, marinades, and baked products. Additionally, ginger tea can be used to make creative drinks like cocktails, smoothies, and syrups with infused flavors.

With its spicy flavor, energizing aroma, and a number of health advantages, ginger is a well-liked herb for herbal tea. Ginger has been valued for centuries for its ability to assist the digestive system, stimulate the immune system, reduce inflammation, and be utilized in a variety of culinary applications. Ginger tea provides a delicious and revitalizing tea-drinking experience, whether you're looking for a warming and energizing beverage, a zesty addition to culinary pleasures, or relief from stomach discomfort. Explore the healing properties of ginger as it enlivens your senses and promotes your overall well-being. Indulge in its fiery warmth.

## Lavender

With its alluring aroma and calming effects, lavender has a well-deserved reputation as one of the most widely used herbs in herbal tea. Lavender tea has been treasured for ages as a calming and therapeutic beverage due to its exquisite flowers and calming scent. We will look at the history, characteristics, health advantages, and various applications of lavender in herbal tea in this section. Lavender continues to enthrall tea enthusiasts all over the world with its rich history and numerous medicinal benefits.

Lavandula angustifolia, the scientific name for lavender, is a flowering plant that is indigenous to the Mediterranean region. Its use dates back to the time of the Egyptians, Greeks, and Romans, among other ancient civilizations. The word "lavender" comes from the Latin verb "lavare," which means "to wash," emphasizing its usage in herbal medicines, fragrances, and bathing rituals. One of the most popular and versatile herbs in herbal therapy, lavender has long been celebrated for its healing abilities.

Lavender tea is well known for its delicate and calming aroma, which produces a tranquil and welcoming atmosphere. The essential oils included in the lavender plant's flowers give the tea a floral and slightly sweet flavor. When brewed, lavender tea emits a soft, calming aroma that is reminiscent of fresh herbs and flowers. Lavender tea is a well-liked option for relaxation, stress alleviation, and increasing general wellbeing because of the delicate flavor and calming aroma.

The capacity of lavender to encourage relaxation and facilitate sound sleep is one of its most well-known advantages. Linalool and linalyl acetate, two compounds found in lavender, exert relaxing and calming effects on the nervous system. In addition to promoting calm and a restful night's sleep, drinking lavender tea can help reduce tension, anxiety, and insomnia. Making a relaxing bedtime routine out of drinking lavender tea will help you relax more.

Due to its capacity to lower stress levels and improve mood, lavender tea is frequently desired. Lavender's aromatic components have a favorable effect on brain chemistry, which helps people feel calm and relaxed. For individuals looking for a natural remedy for stress, tension, and moderate mood disorders, lavender tea is a popular option. Making lavender tea a regular part of your routine might provide you moments of peace and emotional well-being.

It is well known that drinking lavender tea can relieve gastrointestinal discomfort and enhance digestive health. The calming scent and natural ingredients in lavender can ease gastrointestinal symptoms, calm the digestive tract, and lessen bloating. Additionally, the calming effects of lavender tea can aid in reducing stomach muscle tension, which promotes easier digestion and general digestive health.

There are significant advantages of lavender for skincare and attractiveness. Due to its calming and antimicrobial qualities, it is frequently used in natural skincare products including creams, oils, and soaps. When applied topically, lavender tea can be used as a facial steam or rinse to purify the skin, calm inflammation, and support a glowing complexion. Due to its antioxidant characteristics and capacity to promote general skin health, drinking lavender tea may also help you have beautiful skin and hair.

Lavender is used in food preparation in addition to making herbal tea. Lavender's subtle flavor gives a range of foods and drinks a floral, somewhat sweet note. Desserts, baked items, and drinks like lemonades, syrups, and cocktails can all be infused with lavender blossoms. Lavender's distinctive aroma and flavor can enhance dishes when used judiciously.

With its enticing perfume, relaxing qualities, and a variety of health advantages, lavender is a popular herb for herbal tea. Lavender has been cherished for its calming effects, digestive support, skincare advantages, and culinary adaptability from its ancient origins to its current appeal. Lavender tea delivers an appealing and calming tea-drinking experience, whether you're looking for a moment of serenity, a restful night's sleep, or a fragrant infusion to enhance culinary delights. Explore lavender's healing properties and captivating aroma as they enhance your senses and improve your general well-being.

## Lemon balm

With its energizing qualities and vibrant citrus scent, lemon balm has emerged as one of the most popular herbs for herbal tea. Lemon balm tea has been enjoyed for generations as a revitalizing and healing beverage due to its lemony scent and calming properties. We will look at the history, characteristics, health advantages, and various applications of lemon balm in herbal tea in this section. Lemon balm continues to enthrall tea enthusiasts all over the world with its rich history and myriad medicinal benefits.

Lemon balm is a perennial herb that is indigenous to the Mediterranean region and has the scientific name Melissa officinalis. It was highly regarded for its therapeutic benefits and culinary worth in ancient Greece and Rome, where it has a long history of use. The word "Melissa" is a translation of the Greek word for honeybee, emphasizing the plant's allure to bees and the sweetness of its nectar. Lemon balm has long been valued for its calming flavor, zesty aroma, and medicinal uses.

The refreshing and en'rgizing aroma of lemon balm tea, which is reminiscent of fresh lemons and herbs, is much celebrated. Citral and citronellal, two essential oils found in lemon balm leaves, help to give the herb its unique citrus fragrance. The aroma of lemon balm, which is released during the steeping process, enhances the taste of tea. Lemon balm tea has a light flavor with a subtle lemony taste that provides an enjoyable and calming feeling.

The potential of lemon balm to encourage serenity and relaxation is one of its most well-known advantages. Rosmarinic acid and eugenol, two compounds found in lemon balm, have a relaxing impact on the nervous system. The consumption of lemon balm tea can help lower stress levels, foster calmness, and reduce anxiety. It is frequently employed as a natural treatment for agitation, anxiety, and sleep difficulties. A calming ritual can be established and emotional wellbeing supported by incorporating lemon balm tea into your daily routine.

The digestive properties of lemon balm tea and its capacity to calm the gastrointestinal tract are well recognized. It can ease moderate stomach distress, bloating, and discomfort related to the digestive system. The polyphenols and volatile oils found in lemon balm contain carminative and antispasmodic qualities that can help with digestion and reduce gastrointestinal spasms. Drinking lemon balm tea after meals might promote a healthy digestive system and ease digestive issues.

Lemon balm has a long history of being associated to improved memory and cognitive performance. It is thought to improve cognitive function and brain health. Rosmarinic acid and flavonoids, among other antioxidants and substances included in lemon balm, may aid in protecting brain cells from oxidative stress and enhancing cognitive function. Regularly drinking lemon balm tea may improve focus, concentration, and overall cognitive health.

Lemon balm has a reputation for strengthening the immune system because of its antiviral and antioxidant activities. The plant contains substances like ferulic acid and caffeic acid that have antiviral properties against some viruses, including the herpes simplex virus. During times of seasonal immunological problems and possibly for overall immune health, lemon balm tea can be helpful.

Lemon balm is a versatile herb for culinary uses because of its zesty flavor. Lemon balm leaves can be used to infuse cocktails, iced tea, and lemonades to give them a pleasant flavor. It can also be used in salads, marinades, sweets, and herbal syrups, where its delicately lemony flavor enhances a variety of flavors.

With its invigorating aroma, relaxing effects, and numerous health advantages, lemon balm is a beloved herbal tea ingredient. Lemon balm has been valued for its energizing qualities, digestive support, cognitive stimulation, and culinary variety from its ancient origins to its modern-day popularity. Lemon balm tea delivers an attractive and energizing tea-drinking experience, whether you're looking for a moment of serenity, a calming solution for digestion, or a citrus-infused culinary delight. As lemon balm uplifts your senses and aids to your general well-being, welcome the zingy freshness and investigate its therapeutic embrace.

## Rooibos

With its vibrant color, powerful flavor, and an abundance of health advantages, rooibos has become one of the most popular herbs for herbal tea. The leaves of the Aspalathus linearis plant, a native of South Africa, are used to make rooibos tea, which is sometimes referred to as red bush tea. We'll look at the history, characteristics, health advantages, and several applications of rooibos in this section for herbal tea. Rooibos continues to enchant tea enthusiasts all around the world because of its cultural significance and potential therapeutic effects.

South African traditions have a long history of influencing Rooibos tea. Rooibos has been utilized by the indigenous people of the area for a long time as a tasty beverage and for its therapeutic benefits. The plant has been cultivated for many years and only grows in South Africa's Cederberg Mountains. Early in the 20th century, Rooibos achieved recognition on a global scale and has since become a popular herbal tea.

In contrast to other herbal teas, Rooibos tea has a unique flavor character. It has a flavor that is naturally sweet and slightly nutty, and is often referred to as smooth and full-bodied. The bitterness or astringency typically associated with traditional teas is absent from rooibos, in contrast to some herbal teas. Because of this, it is a desirable option for individuals who want a milder and more approachable herbal infusion.

The strong antioxidant content of rooibos tea is one of its main draws. Aspalathin and quercetin are two polyphenols found in rooibos that are potent antioxidants in the body. These compounds improve overall health by battling free radicals, lowering oxidative stress, and reducing inflammation. Regular rooibos tea consumption may strengthen the immune system and provide defense against chronic illnesses.

Rooibos tea has a number of possible health advantages. It is frequently celebrated for its anti-inflammatory qualities, which may lessen inflammatory responses in the body and ease symptoms of arthritis. Additionally, rooibos is thought to enhance cardiovascular health by fostering good circulation and lowering blood pressure. The tea is also naturally devoid of caffeine, making it a good option for anyone trying to cut back on their intake.

Many people drink Rooibos tea because of its calming and soothing properties. It has compounds that interact with the central nervous system to ease tension and promote relaxation. Having a cup of rooibos tea can be a soothing habit that brings you some peace during a hectic day. Its relaxing qualities make it a great option for people looking for a mild, caffeine-free substitute for regular teas.

A hydrating beverage that can help the body stay hydrated generally is rooibos tea. In order to keep your skin healthy, it's important to be adequately hydrated, and rooibos tea can help. The antioxidants in rooibos aid in preventing oxidative skin damage, which may lessen aging symptoms and encourage a young appearance.

In addition to being a popular herbal tea on its own, rooibos may be included into a number of cuisines. Its distinctive flavor complements both sweet and savory foods wonderfully. Iced teas, smoothie bases, as well as baked items and sweets, can all be made with Rooibos tea. Tea enthusiasts can discover the many culinary uses for this unique plant due to its versatility in the kitchen.

Tea enthusiasts are enthralled with Rooibos tea's rich flavor, potential health advantages, and cultural importance, making it a beloved herb for herbal tea. Rooibos has been appreciated for its antioxidant qualities, calming benefits, and culinary diversity since its South African roots and rise to global acclaim. The experience of drinking rooibos tea is wonderful and nourishing, whether you're looking for a moment of relaxation, a tasty, caffeine-free alternative, or a special ingredient for culinary explorations. Rooibos' warmth and richness will enhance your senses and improve your general wellbeing, so embrace it.

## Hibiscus

Hibiscus has become one of the most popular herbs for herbal tea due to its beautiful flowers and tangy flavor. Hibiscus tea, popular for its vibrant colors and tangy flavor, is a light and healthy beverage option. The history, characteristics, health advantages, and several applications of hibiscus in herbal tea will all be discussed in this section. Hibiscus continues to enthrall tea enthusiasts all over the world because of its cultural significance and potential therapeutic benefits.

A flowering plant native to tropical and subtropical climates, the hibiscus is a member of the Malvaceae family. It has long been employed in traditional medical and culinary activities and has cultural importance in many parts of the world. Hibiscus is connected to health, beauty, and joy in many civilizations. It is a well-liked component in herbal tea blends because of its vibrant flowers and tart flavor.

Hibiscus tea is well known for its tart and tangy flavor, which is frequently characterized as pleasant or citrus-like. The hibiscus flower's dried calyces are used to make tea, giving it a vibrant red color and a distinctly tart flavor. Hibiscus tea is a great option for individuals looking for an energizing and revitalizing herbal infusion because of its flavor profile.

The high antioxidant content of hibiscus tea is one of its main draws. Anthocyanins, a class of antioxidant that has many health advantages, are what give hibiscus tea its vibrant red hue. Antioxidants support overall health by shielding the body from oxidative stress and free radicals. Regular hibiscus tea use may strengthen the immune system, lessen inflammation, and improve cellular health.

Many people commend hibiscus tea for its potential cardiovascular advantages. According to studies, hibiscus tea may decrease blood pressure and lower cholesterol. Hibiscus' anthocyanins and other bioactive compounds enhance cardiovascular health by promoting normal blood flow, lowering the risk of heart disease, and lowering blood pressure. Hibiscus tea can be a delectable approach to boost heart health when incorporated into a balanced lifestyle.

Hibiscus tea is a hydrating beverage that can help the body stay hydrated generally. Maintaining healthy bodily processes, such as digestion, circulation, and toxin disposal, requires staying appropriately hydrated. Additionally, hibiscus tea has diuretic qualities that may help remove toxins and support kidney function. Hibiscus tea can be a hydrating and revitalizing way to assist your body's natural cleansing procedures.

Hibiscus tea's tart flavor is not only energizing but also beneficial for a healthy digestive system. Natural enzymes found in hibiscus help break down food and encourage effective digestion. It can ease indigestion, bloating, and digestive discomfort. Additionally, the diuretic effects of hibiscus tea can help to maintain a healthy urinary system and encourage regular bowel motions.

Hibiscus tea offers a wide range of culinary options in addition to its health advantages. It makes a delicious ingredient for preparing energizing drinks, cocktails, and culinary delights due to its tart flavor and brilliant color. Hibiscus tea can be combined with different herbs and spices to make interesting flavor combinations. It can also be used as the base for iced teas, infused into sorbets, added to marinades, and more. Hibiscus tea's adaptability enables tea enthusiasts to experiment and let their culinary imaginations run wild.

A beloved herb for herbal tea, hibiscus tea enchants tea enthusiasts with its vibrant hue, tangy flavor, and potential health advantages. Hibiscus continues to be accepted for its antioxidants, cardiovascular support, digestive assistance, and culinary diversity, in addition to its cultural significance and therapeutic benefits. Hibiscus tea offers a delicious and healthy tea-drinking experience, whether you're looking for a revitalizing beverage, a natural way to support heart health, or an ingredient to enrich culinary creations. Enjoy the hibiscus' vivid splendour and tart charm as it nourishes your senses and improves your general wellbeing.

## Echinacea

With its colorful flowers and great medicinal qualities, echinacea has become one of the most popular herbs for herbal tea. Echinacea tea provides a natural and comprehensive approach to improving general well-being and is widely known for its immune-boosting properties. We will look at the history, characteristics, health advantages, and several applications of echinacea in this section. Echinacea continues to enthrall tea enthusiasts all around the world due to its long history of use by traditional civilizations and modern popularity.

The daisy family includes the genus of blooming plants known as echinacea. Echinacea is a native of North America and has a long history of use as a medicinal herb among indigenous peoples. Native American cultures valued echinacea for its immune-boosting qualities and used it as a treatment for a variety of diseases, including the Plains Indians. Echinacea is now grown and appreciated all over the world because of its possible health advantages.

Echinacea is a well-liked option for people looking for natural ways to enhance their immune system because of its well-known immune-boosting qualities. Flavonoids, polysaccharides, and alkamides, among other active compounds found in the plant, promote the activity of immune cells and strengthen the body's defense mechanisms. Regular echinacea tea drinking may boost the immune system, lessen the severity and length of colds and flu, and improve general health.

Drinking echinacea tea frequently can help with cold and flu symptoms. Echinacea may lessen the severity and duration of upper respiratory tract infections, according to research. Symptoms including a sore throat, a cough, congestion, and weariness can all be alleviated by it. The immune-stimulating effects of echinacea aid the body in fending against bacterial and viral infections, promoting a quicker recovery and a stronger immune system.

Echinacea has immune-enhancing qualities as well as anti-inflammatory actions that can benefit your overall well-being and health. Numerous diseases, such as autoimmune disorders, cardiovascular diseases, and rheumatoid arthritis, are associated with chronic inflammation. The anti-inflammatory components in echinacea may aid in reducing bodily inflammation, fostering a healthy immune response, and maybe lowering the chance of developing chronic inflammatory disorders.

For its therapeutic benefits, echinacea has traditionally been applied topically. Echinacea extracts have been discovered to have antibacterial and wound-healing properties when administered topically. Echinacea tea use may additionally improve internal skin health. Its immune-stimulating and anti-inflammatory characteristics may aid the body's normal healing processes, thereby accelerating wound healing and enhancing skin conditions.

Tea made with echinacea may be very advantageous for respiratory health. It can be able to lessen the signs and symptoms of sinusitis and bronchitis, as well as other respiratory tract diseases. The immune-stimulating and anti-inflammatory characteristics of echinacea may aid in easing respiratory system inflammation, clearing congested airways, and supporting appropriate respiratory function. Echinacea tea can support the respiratory system, speed recovery, and provide respiratory support throughout cold and flu season and when experiencing respiratory symptoms.

In addition to being beneficial for your physical health, echinacea tea can also improve your mental and emotional wellness. Making and drinking warm echinacea tea can be calming and comfortable, aiding in relaxation and stress reduction. By increasing the body's resistance to stress and encouraging a healthy immunological response, echinacea's immune-stimulating properties may further enhance general wellbeing.

As a cherished herbal tea ingredient, echinacea tea enchants tea enthusiasts with its immune-stimulating qualities, historical significance, and potential health advantages. Echinacea continues to be appreciated for its capacity to boost the immune system, lessen cold and flu symptoms, improve respiratory health, promote wound healing, and contribute to general well-being, both in its traditional use by indigenous cultures and in its modern applications. Accept the power of echinacea as it enhances your senses, strengthens your immune system, and aids in your pursuit of holistic health.

**Rosehip**

Rosehip has become one of the most popular herbs for herbal tea because of its exquisite appearance and high nutritional content. Rosehip tea is a popular beverage choice because of its tart flavor and wealth of vitamins and antioxidants. We will look into the history, characteristics, health advantages, and various applications of rosehip in herbal tea in this section. Rosehip continues to enthrall tea enthusiasts all over the world because of its long history as a medicinal plant and its current popularity.

The term "rosehip" refers to the fruit of Rosa spp., or wild rose, plants. After the rose petals fall off, a bulbous, reddish-orange fruit called a rosehip forms. Rosehips have been valued for their therapeutic qualities throughout history. Ancient civilizations, such as the Greeks and Romans, were aware of the medicinal value of rosehip and employed it as a treatment for a variety of illnesses.

Rosehip was also used by Native American cultures for its therapeutic qualities. Rosehip is now grown and cherished all over the world because of its possible health advantages.

Rosehip is loaded with vital vitamins, minerals, and antioxidants, making it an excellent source of nutrition. It has even higher amounts of vitamin C than citrus fruits, making it exceptionally rich in this vitamin. Vitamins A, E, and K, as well as a number of B vitamins, are also present in rosehip. Rosehip is a good source of minerals like calcium, magnesium, phosphorus, and potassium in addition to vitamins. Rosehip is a useful complement to a healthy diet and a nutritious component of herbal tea because of its high nutritional content.

The remarkable antioxidant content of rosehip tea is one of its primary attractions. Antioxidants such as flavonoids, polyphenols, and vitamin C are abundant in rosehips. These antioxidants contribute to overall health by shielding the body from oxidative stress and free radicals. Regular rosehip tea consumption may help to maintain a strong immune system, lower inflammation, and improve cellular health. Antioxidants present in rosehip tea can also maintain healthy skin and fight aging symptoms.

Rosehip tea is well known for enhancing the immune system. The high vitamin C content of rosehips is essential for the immune system's health because it increases the creation of white blood cells, which are better able to fight off infections. Regular consumption of rosehip tea can support overall wellness by boosting the immune system, lowering the risk of contracting common illnesses, and reducing stress.

Rosehip tea has long been used to enhance joint health and reduce the signs and symptoms of inflammatory diseases like arthritis. Rosehip's anti-inflammatory qualities can aid in reducing stiffness, swelling, and joint pain. Rosehip tea's bioactive compounds and antioxidants may also help to maintain and heal joint tissues, promoting overall joint mobility and function.

Rosehip tea has digestive advantages and can improve gut health in general. Tannins and pectin, two naturally occurring components in rosehips, have moderate astringent and relaxing effects that may aid to relieve stomach discomfort and promote good digestion. Constipation, bloating, and indigestion problems can all be treated with rosehip tea. Rosehip tea is ideal for people with sensitive digestive systems because of its mild nature.

In addition to being good for internal health, rosehip tea also nourishes and beautifies the skin. By preventing damage from external elements and fostering collagen synthesis, the antioxidants and vitamins included in rosehip tea promote healthy skin. Regular drinking of rosehip tea may enhance skin suppleness, minimize the appearance of wrinkles and age spots, and promote a more youthful complexion.

Rosehip tea is a beloved herbal tea ingredient that enchants tea enthusiasts with its tart flavor, remarkable nutritional profile, and potential health advantages. Rosehip continues to be valued for its high vitamin C concentration, antioxidant activity, immune-boosting characteristics, support for joint health, digestive assistance, and skin nourishment—from its historical relevance to its present applications. As it improves your tea-drinking experience and contributes to your general wellbeing, embrace the subtle allure and nutrient-rich properties of rosehip.

## Nettle

One of the most popular herbs for herbal tea is nettle, which is known for its prickly leaves and exceptional health benefits. Nettle tea is a popular beverage choice because of its distinctive flavor and medicinal benefits. We will explore the history, characteristics, health advantages, and several applications of nettle in this section for herbal tea. Nettle continues to enthrall tea enthusiasts all over the world due to its long history of use as a medicine plant and current popularity.

Nettle is a perennial plant that thrives in temperate climates all over the world. Its scientific name is Urtica dioica. It has a long history of use in both cooking and traditional medicine. Ancient cultures valued nettle for its therapeutic qualities, notably the Greeks and Romans. Many societies in Europe and Asia, as well as Native American groups, have embraced nettle for its healing properties. Nettle is now widely grown and cherished because of its possible health advantages.

The remarkable nutritional profile of nettle is well known. It contains a lot of vitamins, minerals, and other healthy substances. Along with various B vitamins, nettles also include the vitamins A, C, and K. Additionally, it is a wonderful source of minerals like potassium, calcium, magnesium, and iron. The antioxidants, flavonoids, and plant components that are abundant in nettle also add to its general health-promoting effects. Nettle is a wonderful addition to a healthy diet and a nourishing component of herbal tea because of its high nutritional content.

Nettle tea is frequently consumed for its cleansing and detoxifying effects. Nettle functions as a natural diuretic, increasing urine output and aiding in the body's removal of toxins. It can boost liver and kidney function, which will help the body detoxify. Regular nettle tea consumption may stimulate detoxification, decrease water retention, and cleanse the body.

The ability of nettle tea to reduce allergy symptoms is well known, especially those brought on by seasonal allergies like hay fever. Nettle includes substances that prevent histamine, a major factor in allergic reactions, from being produced. Nettle tea helps ease allergy-related sneezing, nasal congestion, and itching by lowering histamine levels. Additionally, nettle's anti-inflammatory qualities may offer treatment for respiratory illnesses including bronchitis and asthma, promoting good respiratory health.

Nettle tea has long been used to enhance joint health and reduce the signs and symptoms of inflammatory diseases like arthritis. Nettle has anti-inflammatory compounds that can help lessen stiffness, swelling, and joint pain. Nettle tea consumption on a regular basis might enhance joint comfort and mobility.

Nettle tea has advantages for the health and appearance of the skin. By lowering inflammation, calming irritation, and preventing free radical damage, its anti-inflammatory and antioxidant qualities can support healthy skin. Nettle tea may also help in the treatment of skin disorders like psoriasis, dermatitis, and acne. The vitamins and minerals included in nettle maintain a healthy, young complexion by nourishing and rejuvenating the skin.

The digestive system may benefit from nettle tea. It has mild laxative qualities that can aid in encouraging regular bowel motions and relieving constipation. Nettle tea may also help to relieve bloating, improve good digestion, and ease other digestive problems. The anti-inflammatory qualities of nettle may also contribute to the digestive system's general health.

Because of its potential advantages in fostering healthy hair and scalp, nettle tea is frequently applied topically as a hair rinse or included in hair care products. Nettle tea's astringent qualities and vitamins and minerals can aid to strengthen hair follicles, prevent hair loss, and encourage new hair growth. Nettle tea is a healthy, natural remedy for hair care and can help with scalp issues including dandruff and an oily scalp.

With its distinctive flavor, versatility, and potential health advantages, nettle tea is a beloved herb for herbal tea. Nettle continues to be appreciated for its cleansing abilities, allergy relief, joint support, skin health benefits, digestive aid, and hair care advantages—from its historical significance to its present applications. Accept the extraordinary benefits of nettle as it improves your tea-drinking experience and adds to your overall health and vitality.

# Chapter IV

## Preparing Herbal Infusions

### Infusion techniques for different herbs

The infusion method is essential for obtaining the tastes, scents, and medicinal benefits of many herbs in the realm of herbal tea. To obtain ideal absorption and make a wonderful cup of herbal tea, each herb needs a different strategy. This section will examine the art of infusion procedures for various herbs, the influences on infusion, and how to master them to maximize the benefits of herbal tea. We will explore the methods that let us enjoy the richness and advantages of various herbal blends, from light infusions to decoctions.

Herbs are steeped in hot water to extract the desired characteristics, a process known as infusion. The outcome is a tasty and aromatic beverage because it enables the water to absorb the flavors, colors, and beneficial compounds from the herbs. The temperature, steeping period, and water-to-herb ratio are crucial variables that affect the outcome of the infusion.

The delicate tastes and aromatic components of delicate herbs, like chamomile and peppermint, must be preserved by using mild infusion processes. The soothing and calming effects of chamomile can be released when the herb is steeped for 5-7 minutes at a temperature of about 200°F (93°C), which is optimum. For its energizing and refreshing flavor, peppermint, on the other hand, benefits from a slightly higher temperature of 212°F (100°C) and a shorter steeping duration of 3–5 minutes.

To extract their potent flavors and beneficial advantages, robust plants like ginger and cinnamon need longer infusions at higher temperatures. Ginger, which is renowned for its spiciness and warming properties, can be steeped for 7–10 minutes at 212°F (100°C) to release its aromatic compounds and medicinal properties. Cinnamon benefits from a similar temperature and steeping period to fully reveal its rich flavor and potential health benefits due to its sweet and aromatic nature.

Woody herbs like rosemary and thyme require infusions to draw out their fragrant and essential oils. These herbs should be steeped at a higher temperature of 212°F (100°C) for 7–10 minutes to properly extract their flavor and therapeutic effects. You can sip these infusions on their own or combine them with other herbs to make distinctive herbal tea blends.

To maintain their delicate flavors and scents, floral herbs like lavender and rose petals create infusions that are delicate and fragrant. These herbs should be steeped at a lower temperature, around 180–190°F (82–88°C), as bitterness can develop at higher temperatures. The water may absorb the floral essence by steeping for 5-7 minutes, producing a calming and fragrant tea.

To extract their potent tastes and healthful ingredients, root and bark herbs like licorice root and cacao nibs need to be steeped for longer periods of time at higher temperatures. To release the complex flavors and potential health benefits of these herbs, a steeping temperature of 212°F (100°C) and a steeping period of 10 to 15 minutes are advised. You can sip these infusions on their own or combine them with other herbs to make elaborate and decadent herbal teas.

Some herbal blends include hard plant components like roots, barks, and seeds that need to be prepared using a distinct process called decoction. In order to thoroughly extract the tastes and medicinal benefits of the herbs, decoction entails boiling the herbs in water for a longer period of time. Astragalus root and burdock root are two herbs that are frequently prepared in this manner. The water is boiled with the herbs for at least 20 to 30 minutes to allow the water to absorb the flavor of the hard plant components. Decoctions are frequently employed as the foundation for herbal treatments since they are frequently stronger and more concentrated than standard infusions.

Exploring the various flavors, scents, and health advantages of various herbs in herbal tea requires mastering the art of infusion procedures. Every herb, from delicate ones like chamomile and peppermint to powerful ones like ginger and cinnamon, requires a certain method to produce the ideal infusion. We can make amazing herbal teas that enchant our senses and encourage well-being by comprehending the characteristics and qualities of numerous herbs as well as the variables that affect infusion. Embrace the exploration of herbal tea, and enjoy the amazing flavors and health advantages that infusion methods provide to your cup.

## Water temperature and steeping time guidelines

Water temperature and steeping time are two essential elements that have a big impact on the final product. Brewing herbal tea is an art that takes meticulous attention to detail. These components control how the flavors, smells, and healthy compounds of the herbs are extracted, producing a balanced and pleasurable cup of herbal tea. We will discuss the significance of steeping time and water temperature in brewing herbal tea in this section, offering tips and insights to help you make the ideal cup every time.

In order to extract the right flavors and characteristics from herbal tea, water temperature is essential. To maximize their extraction while preventing the extraction of undesirable components that could cause bitterness or loss of delicate flavors, different herbs require varying water temperatures.

For powerful and robust herbal infusions, boiling water, often at 212°F (100°C), is the ideal temperature. Higher temperatures help to fully extract the flavor and therapeutic benefits of herbs like ginger, cinnamon, and licorice root. A powerful and energizing cup of herbal tea can be made by steeping these herbs in boiling water for 7 to 10 minutes.

Water temperatures slightly below boiling are typically between 190°F (88°C) and 205°F (96°C) for most herbal infusions. The risk of over-extraction or bitterness is reduced while still allowing for effective extraction at these temperatures.

Lower water temperatures between 190°F (88°C) and 200°F (93°C) are beneficial for delicate herbs like chamomile, lavender, and rose petals as well as floral mixtures. The flavors and subtle fragrances of these herbs can slowly develop over the course of 5-7 minutes when steeped in water that is between these two temperatures, producing a calming and fragrant cup of herbal tea.

Water temperatures between 200°F (93°C) and 205°F (96°C) are advised for the majority of herbal teas, including well-known herbs like peppermint, nettle, and lemon balm. These herbs can extract their flavors, scents, and possible health benefits while retaining a harmonious and pleasing taste by steeping them for 5-7 minutes.

Another crucial element that affects how strong and flavorful a herbal tea is the amount of time it is steeped. Depending on the herbs used and individual preferences, steeping times vary.

Chamomile and mint are examples of delicate herbs and herbal mixes that benefit from shorter steeping durations of 3–5 minutes. A milder infusion can be produced by steeping herbs for a shorter amount of time, keeping their subtle undertones and avoiding any potential harshness.

The typical steeping period for herbal infusions is 5-7 minutes. This time frame enables a balanced extraction of flavors and medicinal qualities from the herbs, producing a cup of herbal tea that is both flavorful and satisfying. This group of herbs includes lavender, nettle, and lemon balm, which benefit from a modest steeping duration to produce the best flavor profiles.

Longer steeping times are beneficial for some herbal teas, notably those having roots, barks, or seeds. The full spectrum of flavors and potential health benefits of herbs like dandelion root, burdock root, and astragalus root may require steeping for 10-15 minutes or longer. It's crucial to keep in mind, though, that a lengthier steeping may produce an infusion that is stronger and more concentrated, which might not be to everyone's taste.

Fundamental components of brewing herbal tea include water temperature and steeping duration, which have a big impact on the final beverage's flavor, aroma, and medicinal characteristics. You can unleash the full power of each infusion and provide a harmonious and pleasurable tea drinking experience by knowing the ideal temperature and time for various herbs. Try out different combinations, modify the settings to your liking, and set out on a discovery adventure as you indulge in the complex flavors and health benefits of herbal tea prepared with care and accuracy.

## Blending herbs for customized flavors

When it comes to experimenting with flavors and personalizing a drink, herbal tea offers a plethora of options. The technique of combining herbs is one of the secrets to making distinctive and delicious herbal teas. We may tailor a symphony of flavors, fragrances, and therapeutic advantages from combining several herbs to suit our own preferences and needs. We will delve into the concepts, methods, and imaginative possibilities that enable us to create unique and entrancing brews as we explore the art of blending herbs for customized flavors in herbal tea.

In order to develop a flavor profile that is harmonious, blending herbs entails the careful selection and blending of numerous botanical elements. To make harmonious and satisfying tea blends, it is important to comprehend the basic concepts of herbal mixing. These guidelines include taking into account the flavor intensity, opposing and complimentary flavors, and the expected medicinal effects of the plants.

It is essential to take into account the strength of each herb's flavor while mixing herbs. While some have more delicate flavors, other herbs have strong, dominating flavors. We may make a flavorful blend that is well-rounded and nuanced by harmonizing the flavors and stacking them in the proper amounts. A tea with the ideal combination of minty, flowery, and citrusy overtones, for instance, can be made by combining peppermint, chamomile, and lemon balm.

Herbs and complimentary or opposing flavors can be used to create fascinating and scrumptious flavor combinations. The floral tones of complementary fragrances like lavender and chamomile are enhanced by one another, resulting in a calming and pleasant combination. Contrasting flavors, like as ginger and lemongrass, on the other hand, give the mixture a zesty and spicy kick and add complexity and depth.

Herbal mixtures can be created for both their tastes and their medicinal properties. Every herb has special qualities that can enhance general health. For instance, nettle, dandelion root, and burdock root can be combined to make a purifying and cleansing mixture that promotes liver function. We can modify our blends to address particular requirements or improve particular elements of our health by being aware of the medicinal characteristics of the herbs.

The ratios of the herbs in a blend are quite important in creating the flavor profile as a whole. By experimenting with various ratios, we may adjust the flavor balance to our tastes. Starting with lesser amounts of stronger herbs and progressively adjusting their proportions until the appropriate flavor is obtained is frequently helpful. This iterative blending and tasting procedure enables a unique and tailored tea experience.

Herb blending offers a platform for original thought and expression. You may develop distinctive blends that showcase your distinct taste preferences and sense of fashion. Try experimenting with herbs that have a special meaning for you, like hibiscus, rose petals, or cinnamon, and blend them with other herbs to make a concoction that is genuinely unique to you. As you investigate the limitless potential of herbal alchemy, let your imagination lead the way.

It is helpful to keep track of your mixes and the ratios used as you begin your herbal blending journey. By doing this, you can improve your recipes and recreate effective blends in the future. Additionally, keeping track of the tastes, scents, and medicinal properties of each mix helps one comprehend the dynamics of various herbs and facilitates the gradual development of more complex and well-balanced blends.

The community surrounding herbal tea mixing is active and welcoming. Speaking with other tea lovers, herbalists, or members of online forums can provide you ideas, pointers, and a place to share your own blends. You can increase your expertise and gain access to fresh concepts and flavor fusions by taking part in tea tastings, workshops, and blending competitions.

Herbal tea blending is an art form that encourages us to explore, experiment, and produce distinctive blends that are catered to our specific tastes and preferences. We may create blends that are not only delicious but also healthy for the body and spirit by comprehending the principles of herbal mixing, taking flavor intensity, complimentary and contrasting flavors, and therapeutic effects into consideration. Discover the fun of creating unique herbal teas that will inspire and delight you as you embark on the road of herbal alchemy.

## Making iced herbal tea

Nothing is more refreshing than a big glass of iced tea when the weather is high and the sun is out. While traditional black or green tea is frequently thought of when thinking of iced tea, the world of herbal tea offers a variety of flavors and health advantages that can be savored over ice. In this section, we'll explore the art of preparing iced herbal tea, from picking the best herbs to using inventive brewing methods and flavorings. Prepare to set out on a voyage filled with enticing and energizing iced herbal teas that will quench your thirst and awaken your senses.

The choice of herbs is important while brewing iced herbal tea. Choose herbs that have flavorful, refreshing undertones to go with iced beverages. Mint, hibiscus, lemongrass, and fruit-infused herbs like raspberry and peach are some of the often used options. These herbs give your iced tea a flavor boost and a hint of sweetness, making the drink incredibly refreshing.

Making iced herbal tea by using the cold brewing technique is very common since it gently absorbs the flavors and scents from the herbs without using hot water. Put your preferred herbs in a pitcher of cold water, cover it, and refrigerate it overnight or at least for four to six hours to make cold brew herbal tea. A smooth, naturally sweet infusion is the end result, which is ideal for sipping on a hot summer day.

Another method for creating iced herbal tea involves brewing it hot and then quickly cooling it. If you want to enjoy your herbal tea right away rather than wait for the long extraction of cold brewing, this approach is great. Simply steep your herbal tea in boiling water for the advised amount of time. After it has been brewed, pour the tea over an ice-filled pitcher to quickly cool it. By using this technique, you can immediately experience the herbal flavors while preserving the cool, refreshing sensation of an iced beverage.

The actual art of creating iced herbal tea can be found in the creation of tasty infusions. Combine several herbs to create interesting flavor combinations. For instance, steep hibiscus and orange peel for a tart and vivid iced tea, or combine mint and lemon verbena for a zesty and cooling blend. The choices are unlimited, and you may create distinctive and energizing blends that match your taste preferences by combining herbs, fruits, and spices.

Consider natural sweeteners like honey, agave syrup, or stevia to give your iced herbal tea a hint of sweetness. The flavors of the herbal infusion are enhanced by these choices without being overpowered. Slices of fresh fruit, such lemon, lime, or berries, can also be added to iced tea to give it an extra taste boost and a more pleasing presentation.

The enjoyment of iced herbal tea is significantly influenced by presentation. Think about adding fresh herbs, lemon slices, or edible flowers as a garnish for your iced tea. These minor adjustments enhance the aesthetic appeal and increase the allure of your drink. To further improve the overall visual and infuse subtle flavors as the ice melts, think about adding flavored or decorative ice cubes, such as freezing berries or herb leaves in the ice cubes.

There are numerous methods to serve iced herbal tea to accommodate various tastes and situations. For gatherings or parties, serve your refreshing concoction in stylish pitchers or tall glasses filled with ice. Add soda water or tonic water on top of your iced tea for a fizzy and effervescent treat to give it a sparkling twist. For a pleasant flavor fusion, you may even try blending iced herbal tea with fruit juices or kombucha.

Even though freshly made iced herbal tea is ideal, you might have leftover infusion. To ensure its freshness, store any leftover tea in the refrigerator in a container that is well closed. To ensure the finest flavor and quality, it is typically advised to drink homemade iced tea within 2-3 days of making it. Use your best judgment, though, and always look for signs of decomposition before consuming.

Making iced herbal tea turns into a cool and delightful task when the summer heat approaches. You can make a variety of energizing and delectable iced herbal teas by carefully choosing your herbs, experimenting with various brewing techniques, and adding inventive flavor combinations. The world of iced herbal tea will calm your senses, soothe your thirst, and take you on a journey of refreshing and energizing flavors.

# Chapter V

# Enhancing Your
# Herbal Tea Experience

**Adding sweeteners and flavorings**

The flavors of herbal tea are varied and pleasant on their own, but occasionally a dash of sweetness or an extra flavor punch can elevate the tea-drinking experience to new heights. Herbal tea can be given a unique taste by adding sweeteners and flavorings that are tailored to each person's preferences. We will go into the realm of herbal tea sweeteners and flavorings in this section, looking at different possibilities, their influence on flavor and scent, and how they might improve how much you enjoy your favorite brew.

Natural sweeteners are frequently preferred over refined sugar when it comes to sweetening herbal tea because of their perceived health advantages. Honey, agave syrup, maple syrup, and stevia are examples of natural sweeteners that offer sweetness without the negative health effects of processed sugar. These sweeteners offer additional nutritional benefits and potential health advantages in addition to a pleasing taste.

The natural sweetener honey is widely-liked and versatile, and it goes well with many herbal teas. Depending on the type of honey, it offers a distinctive flavor profile that can range from delicate and floral to rich and robust. Honey's viscosity makes it simple to dissolve in hot tea, distributing sweetness throughout the liquid. Honey is a popular addition to calming herbal teas like chamomile or lavender because of its antimicrobial and calming qualities.

The agave plant yields agave syrup, which is frequently used as a vegan-friendly sweetener. It pairs well with herbal teas without overpowering their subtle undertones due to its mild, slightly caramel-like flavor. Because agave syrup easily dissolves in hot or cold beverages, it is a practical addition to both hot and iced herbal teas. Its low glycemic index makes it a good option for people who keep an eye on their blood sugar levels.

Herbal teas gain a special and distinctive sweetness from the addition of maple syrup, which is made from the sap of maple trees. When combined with powerful herbs like cinnamon or ginger, maple syrup gives the tea a depth and complexity that is enhanced by its rich and earthy flavor. A versatile option for sweetening hot or iced herbal teas, maple syrup pairs well with both warm and cool herbal infusions.

Stevia is a popular sugar alternative because it has no calories and is derived from plants. Only a small amount is required to sweeten herbal tea because it is derived from the stevia plant's leaves and is significantly sweeter than sugar. Stevia offers a natural sweetness without adding calories or having an effect on blood sugar levels, making it a great option for people managing diabetes or limiting their calorie consumption.

Although herbal teas already have a variety of flavors, adding more flavorings can elevate them to new levels. Flavorings can be used to improve already-present flavors, give them a twist, or make novel combinations. Here are a few preferred flavoring choices to take into account:

Herbal teas can be given a lively and energizing touch by sprinkling on some citrus zest, such lemon, lime, or orange. The oils in the zest give the tea fresh, zesty flavors that balance the herbal undertones.

A little bit of spice can make an ordinary herbal tea into an enthralling sensory experience. Common spices like cinnamon, cardamom, ginger, or cloves can enhance the tea's flavor profile by bringing warmth, depth, and complexity. Find your ideal blend by experimenting with various spice blends.

Herbal teas can be given a delicate and fragrant touch by adding floral essences like rose water, jasmine extract, or lavender oil. These tastes give the tea a subtly floral undertone, making it calming and aromatic to drink.

By adding more herbs to your tea, you can enhance the herbal experience. A chamomile infusion, for instance, tastes revitalizing and refreshing when fresh mint is added. To develop distinctive flavor profiles, explore with herbs like lemongrass, basil, or rosemary.

Striking a balance is crucial when enhancing herbal tea with sweeteners and flavorings. Start with modest amounts and gradually increase or decrease as desired. Each herb has an own natural flavor profile, and based on those characteristics, certain plants may need less or more sweetening or flavoring. Try several combinations and conduct taste tests to find the ideal one that will enhance herbal tea without overpowering it.

You can explore new dimensions of flavor and aroma by incorporating sweeteners and flavorings into herbal tea, which allows you personalize your tea-drinking experience. The use of flavorings like citrus zest, spices, floral essences, and herbal infusions opens up a world of culinary options, while natural sweeteners like honey, agave syrup, maple syrup, and stevia provide healthier alternatives to refined sugar. You can transform your herbal tea into a delicious and unique sensory experience that tantalizes your taste buds and awakens your senses with a focused approach and a spirit of experimentation. Cheers to the craft of making a drink better.

## Pairing herbal tea with food

Herbal teas come in a wide variety of flavors, scents, and health advantages. But did you know that herbal tea can also make a great mealtime beverage? Herbal tea can enhance flavors, cleanse the palate, and produce a pleasant dining experience, much as wine pairs well with some dishes. The ideas, methods, and inventive combinations that enable tea and cuisine to dance together in perfect harmony will all be covered in this section as we investigate the art of pairing herbal tea with food.

Understanding the flavor profiles of both herbal teas and food is crucial before getting into the art of pairings. A wide range of flavors, including floral, lemony, earthy, and spicy undertones, can be found in herbal teas. Similar to this, distinct flavor profiles of food, such as sweet, savory, spicy, and sour, can be classified. We may start to develop flavorful combinations by figuring out which flavors predominate in both the tea and the food.

To combine herbal tea with food, one strategy is to look for complementing flavors. For instance, a delicate and light dessert like vanilla panna cotta can be combined with a floral herbal tea like chamomile. The delicate sweetness of the dessert and the flowery undertones of the tea combine to make a harmonious and sophisticated dish. Similar to how berry-infused hibiscus, a fruity herbal tea, can be matched with a summer fruit salad to bring out the fruity flavors and provide a cool aspect to the dish.

Contrasting pairings bring together flavors with different attributes to produce an intriguing interplay of taste sensations. For instance, a creamy and light cuisine like coconut curry might be combined with a spicy herbal tea like ginger. In contrast to the richness of the curry, the spiciness of the tea stimulates the palate and adds complexity to the overall dining experience. With each sip and bite, contrasting pairings can produce an interesting combination of flavors and textures that entices the taste senses.

Herbal teas can help to clear the palate, especially when consumed with fatty or rich foods. Some herbal teas, like peppermint or lemongrass, have refreshing and energizing properties that can help clear the palate between meals and get it ready for the next flavor experience. This is especially useful when dining on multiple courses or switching from one dish to another. The taste buds can be reset with a sip of cooling herbal tea, restoring the senses for the upcoming culinary journey.

It can be interesting to think about the regional associations between herbal teas and foods when exploring pairings. For instance, the flavorful spices and complex flavors of dishes like tagines and couscous are complemented by the traditional Moroccan mint tea, which is a perfect match with North African cuisine. Similar to this, Asian herbal teas, such as jasmine or chrysanthemum tea, can be combined with meals that are inspired by Asian cuisine to enhance the flavors and produce a well-rounded dining experience.

The temperature and intensity of both the tea and the dish should be taken into account when combining herbal tea with food. Stronger teas can compete with bolder, more intense flavors, while lighter, more delicate teas combine well with lighter meals. Consider the food's and the tea's temperature as well. When served with hot or spicy food, cold herbal teas can be revitalizing since they offer a temperature contrast that enhances the overall dining experience.

Herbal tea and meal pairing is a skill that promotes creativity and exploration. Don't be scared to experiment with unusual pairings and go from the norm. To provide a distinctive and intriguing smoky aspect to the dinner, a smoky herbal tea like lapsang souchong can be matched with grilled meats or savory barbecued meals. The key to finding intriguing and surprising pairings is to trust your palate, be open to new experiences, and let your creativity lead the way.

Herbal tea stands out as a diverse and interesting beverage that can improve the flavors and textures of food in the world of culinary delights. Herbal tea has the ability to raise the dining experience to new heights through complementing pairings, contrasting combinations, palate-cleansing effects, or regional associations. One can set out on a path of harmonizing sips and bites by comprehending the flavor profiles of the tea and the food, taking temperature and intensity into account, embracing experimentation and creativity, and so on. As a celebration of flavor, scent, and the thrill of culinary exploration, raise your teacup and toast the art of pairing herbal tea with food.

## Herbal tea for relaxation and stress relief

Finding moments of relaxation and stress reduction is crucial for sustaining a healthy and balanced lifestyle in today's fast-paced and demanding society. The calming ritual of drinking herbal tea can be one way to find peace. Herbal teas have long been celebrated for their meditative qualities, delicate flavors, and medicinal uses. We will examine the technique of using herbal tea as a tool for relaxation and stress relief in this section, as well as the science behind it, the various plants that are recognized for their soothing effects, and the traditions that can improve the experience.

Flavonoids, antioxidants, and essential oils are just a few of the different ingredients that give herbal teas their calming and stress-relieving properties. These compounds interact with hormones, neurotransmitters, and receptors in the body to promote relaxation, lessen anxiety, and calm the nervous system. We can better appreciate herbal tea's medicinal advantages if we are aware of the scientific rationale underlying its calming effects.

One of the most popular and extensively utilized plants for relaxing is chamomile. It is a well-liked option for encouraging sound sleep and lowering anxiety because of its mild, floral aroma and calming qualities. Chamomile tea reduces stress through interacting with GABA receptors in the brain, which has a soothing effect. Having a cup of chamomile tea before bed or when you're feeling stressed might help you feel calm and relaxed.

With its distinct aroma and beautiful purple flowers, lavender not only attracts our senses but also has amazing calming properties. It is well known that drinking lavender tea can help you unwind, reduce stress, and get a better night's sleep. Lavender is a great option for anyone looking for a moment of peace and tranquillity because studies have proven that its aroma lowers tension and anxiety levels.

Lemon balm is highly regarded for its ability to relieve tension because of its vibrant lemon flavor and aroma. This plant has compounds that interact with brain receptors to reduce anxiety and promote calm. During stressful times, lemon balm tea can be a wonderful companion, assisting in regaining equilibrium and relaxation.

While peppermint is frequently thought of as having energizing and invigorating properties, it also has relaxing properties. Because of its cooling properties, peppermint tea can help reduce stress and encourage relaxation. Peppermint is a great option for anyone looking for relief from both physical and mental stress because it contains menthol, which has relaxing effects on the muscles.

Adaptogenic plants should also be included in addition to specific herbs known to promote calm. Adaptogens like ashwagandha, rhodiola, and holy basil function by assisting the body's ability to withstand and adapt to stress. By regulating the stress response system, these herbs can enhance general wellbeing and calmness. A comprehensive approach to relaxation and stress relief can be achieved by incorporating adaptogenic herbs into herbal tea blends.

When paired with mindfulness exercises, drinking herbal tea can become a potent ritual for reducing stress and promoting relaxation. The calming effects of herbal tea can be increased by making a calm and serene setting, sipping slowly and deliberately, concentrating on the aroma and flavor, and employing deep breathing exercises. Drinking tea mindfully helps us stay fully in the present, which promotes relaxation and a sense of inner serenity.

It can be fun to make your own herbal tea blends to enhance the relaxation process. Chamomile, lavender, lemon balm, and other calming herbs can be combined to form a synergistic mixture that encourages profound relaxation. By experimenting with various ratios and blends of herbs, we may customize the tea to meet our preferences and requirements and so maximize its calming effects.

Finding times of relaxation and stress release is essential for our wellbeing in a society where expectations and stresses are constant. Herbal tea is a useful resource in our quest for serenity because of its calming effects, mild flavors, and therapeutic advantages. The world of herbal tea offers a wide variety of herbs with calming characteristics, from chamomile to lavender, lemon balm to peppermint. We may create a haven of calm within a simple cup of herbal tea by comprehending the science underlying the calming properties of particular herbs, studying those herbs, and applying mindful practices. Therefore, take a deep breath, prepare a soothing blend, and experience the tranquility and peace that herbal tea offers.

## Herbal tea for specific health conditions

Since ancient times, herbal tea has been used as a home remedy for a variety of illnesses. Herbal teas provide a mild and all-encompassing method of improving wellbeing because they are filled with healthy compounds and therapeutic characteristics. In this section, we'll examine the potential of herbal tea to treat a variety of illnesses, from digestive problems and sleeplessness to respiratory health and immune support. We can use the power of nature to support our general health and vitality by becoming aware of the specific advantages of certain herbs.

Bloating, indigestion, and other digestive problems can significantly lower our quality of life. Fortunately, a number of herbs provide comfort and support good digestion. It is well known that peppermint tea can calm an upset stomach, reduce gas, and lessen symptoms of irritable bowel syndrome (IBS). Ginger tea helps with digestion, lessens motion sickness, and soothes gastrointestinal discomfort because of its anti-inflammatory and carminative effects. Another great option for promoting digestion, reducing bloating, and calming infant colic is fennel tea.

Our overall well-being and health may suffer if we are unable to get a good night's sleep. Herbal teas can be used as a mild and all-natural way to encourage relaxation and enhance the quality of your sleep. Because of its relaxing effects, chamomile tea can help lower anxiety and promote a state of relaxation that is beneficial to sleep. Another popular choice is valerian root tea, which works as a mild sedative to promote deeper sleep and help with sleep onset. Another well-known benefit of passionflower tea is its capacity to encourage relaxation and lessen the symptoms of insomnia.

Immune system health is essential for preventing disease and remaining healthy. Our immune systems can benefit naturally from herbal drinks. Echinacea tea, which is made from the vibrant purple coneflower, is well known for boosting the immune system and preventing infections and colds. It has been demonstrated that elderberry tea, which is high in antioxidants and vitamins, supports immune function and lessens the intensity and duration of cold and flu symptoms. The astragalus plant's root is used to make the tea that can boost immunity and ward off respiratory infections.

Herbal teas can assist to relieve respiratory disorders like coughs, colds, and congestion. Thyme tea can aid with coughs, bronchitis, and congestion due to its expectorant and antispasmodic characteristics. The calming properties of licorice root tea can help soothe sore throats and support respiratory health. Since ancient times, mullein tea, made from the leaves and flowers of the mullein plant, has been used to treat respiratory problems, such as coughs and asthma symptoms.

In the fast-paced world of today, controlling stress and anxiety is crucial to keeping one's mental and emotional health. Teas made from herbs can have a calming and soothing effect that can help reduce tension and encourage relaxation. With its delicate floral aroma, lavender tea has long been used to ease nervous tension, soothe the body, and promote peace. With its light sedative effects, lemon balm tea can boost mood and lessen stress. Holy basil tea, also known as Tulsi tea, is highly regarded in Ayurvedic medicine for its adaptogenic characteristics, which support a sense of balance and aid in the body's ability to adapt to stress.

Herbal teas that target certain issues including menstrual cramps, hormone imbalances, and menopause symptoms can help women's health. Tea made from red raspberry leaves has long been used to strengthen the uterus and lessen menstruation pain. Traditional Chinese Medicine frequently use dong quai tea, which is made from the root of the Angelica sinensis plant, to control menstrual cycles and lessen menstruation pain. The ability of black cohosh tea to reduce menopause symptoms like hot flashes and mood swings is well known.

Additionally, joint pain, inflammation, and muscular discomfort can all be alleviated with herbal teas. Turmeric tea contains curcumin, a substance with potent anti-inflammatory properties that is produced from the bright yellow spice. With its warming properties, ginger tea can help lessen joint pain and inflammation brought on by diseases like arthritis. Devil's claw tea, made from the devil's claw plant's root, has been used for centuries to treat pain and inflammation in the muscles and joints.

An all-natural and holistic method of treating particular medical conditions is herbal tea. Herbal teas offer a gentle and effective way to improve our well-being, from supporting respiratory health and promoting digestive health to enhancing sleep quality and boosting the immune system. We may harness the regenerative force of nature to meet our individual health demands by learning the targeted advantages of various herbs and incorporating them into our daily routines. So why not enjoy the journey to better health and vitality while sipping on a warm cup of herbal tea?

# Chapter IV

## Exploring Herbal Tea Recipes

**Refreshing herbal tea recipes**

There is nothing better than a cool herbal tea for satisfying your thirst and revive your senses while the sun shines bright and the temperature rises. Herbal teas are a delicious and nutritious substitute for sweetened beverages since they are bursting with flavor, have energizing scents, and have a variety of health advantages. We'll set off on an explorational voyage as we learn about several hydrating herbal tea recipes in this section. These recipes, which range from fruity infusions to zesty blends, will not only tempt your taste buds but also offer a cool respite during hot summer days.

Utilize this recipe for a cooling herbal tea to embrace the zingy flavors of citrus fruits. In a pitcher, mix fresh orange, lemon, and lime slices with a few mint leaves. Add boiling water, then wait a few minutes as the flavors meld. After the tea has cooled, filter it and serve it over ice. Your senses will be awakened by the zesty perfume and tart flavor, which will leave you feeling revitalized.

With this colorful herbal tea recipe, you may celebrate the deliciousness of summer berries. Strawberries, raspberries, and blueberries, along with other berries, can be combined fresh or frozen in a pot. For a fragrant twist, add a few fresh basil or mint sprigs. The berries and herbs should be covered with hot water, and the combination should steep for 10 minutes or so. Tea should be strained and served with ice. A delicious and revitalizing beverage will be produced by the explosion of berry flavors and the delicate herbal overtones.

With the help of this exotic herbal tea recipe, you may escape to a tropical paradise. Hibiscus flowers should first be steeped in hot water until the solution turns a deep red color. Add pineapple pieces, mango chunks, and a fresh basil or lemongrass leaf. After a few minutes of flavor infusion, filter the tea, then chill it in the refrigerator. You'll be transported to a cool oasis by the mango, pineapple, and hibiscus in this tropical concoction.

Enjoy this enticing herbal tea recipe and the revitalizing blend of cold melon and stimulating mint. A ripe honeydew melon should be pureed in a blender until smooth. A good handful of fresh mint leaves should be added after you pour the purée into a pitcher. Add cooled water to the pitcher and swirl thoroughly. In the refrigerator, give the flavors some time to mingle. With a mint sprig as a garnish, serve the tea over ice. A refreshing and hydrated sensation will be provided by the crisp melon flavor combined with the minty freshness.

Enjoy the utmost in refreshment with this recipe for refreshing cucumber herbal tea. Cucumber slices should be placed in a pitcher of ice water. Add some lemon or lime juice for an extra zesty kick. You can optionally add a few fresh dill or mint sprigs for taste. For a few hours, let the mixture steep in the refrigerator. Tea should be strained and served over ice with a slice of cucumber or a fresh herb sprig as a garnish. On warm summer days, the moisturizing qualities of the cucumber mixed with the citrus tang and herbal undertones will quench your thirst and cool you off.

With this classy recipe, you can enjoy the delicate and alluring flavors of flowery herbal teas. Combine dried rose petals, chamomile flowers, and a few lavender buds in a teapot. Add hot water to the mixture, then let it steep for a short while. Pour the tea over ice after straining and allowing it to cool. A relaxing and elegant beverage will be produced by the floral aroma and delicate flavors.

Herbal teas provide a wide range of energizing possibilities when the temperatures rise and the need for cool drinks increases. These herbal tea blends offer a wide range of flavors and scents to please any palette, from the zingy citrus splash to the sweet berry explosion, the tropical paradise to the minty melon, the cucumber chiller to the flowery elegance. You can take advantage of herbal teas' positive effects on your health while also treating yourself to these energizing mixtures as part of your daily routine. Grab your favorite herbs, fruits, and a pitcher, then use these lovely herbal tea recipes to go out on a voyage of flavor and refreshment. Toast to summertime drinking!

## Herbal tea blends for different moods

Teas made from herbs have long been prized for their calming, uplifting, and rebalancing effects on our bodies and brains. We may develop distinctive and delicious mixtures using the art of herb mixing that are tailored to our individual moods and requirements. We will look at a variety of herbal tea mixes intended to improve our mental health in this section. These herbal mixtures offer a cozy and tasty approach to support our fluctuating moods throughout the day, ranging from peaceful blends for relaxation to energizing drinks for energy.

A cup of herbal tea can be a calming balm for our tired hearts during times of stress and anxiety. Consider combining chamomile, lavender, and lemon balm to foster calmness and relaxation. The relaxing effects of chamomile help to reduce stress and calm the nervous system. While lemon balm offers a delicate lemon flavor and works as a natural mood enhancer, lavender gives a floral scent and encourages relaxation.

Certain herbs can be the ideal pick-me-up when we need an energy and mental clarity boost. Use herbs like ginseng, peppermint, and rosemary to create a combination. The adaptogenic qualities of ginseng are well known for helping to reduce fatigue and increase focus. While rosemary improves mental clarity and alertness, peppermint awakens the senses and gives a revitalizing energy boost.

We frequently look for a warm, comforting cup of herbal tea on chilly days or in pleasant evenings. Combine cinnamon, ginger, and cloves for this. Cinnamon boosts circulation and offers comfort by adding a sweet and sour flavor. Cloves add a rich, aromatic flavor that promotes feelings of comfort and satisfaction, while ginger offers warmth and aids in digestion.

Our bodies could benefit from a reviving and detoxifying herbal blend after a hard day or a time of excess. Use plants like burdock root, nettle, and dandelion. Dandelion supports kidney health and aids in detoxification by acting as a natural diuretic. Burdock root assists with liver purification and boosts general vitality, while nettle is high in antioxidants and aids in system cleansing.

Certain herbs can help elevate our spirits when we need a boost of joy and optimism. Use herbs like hibiscus, lemon verbena, and St. John's Wort to make a combination. St. John's Wort is well known for its abilities to elevate mood and foster emotions of happiness and wellbeing. Hibiscus provides a tart and sour flavor that awakens the senses, while lemon verbena adds a zesty accent and uplifts the mood.

Herbal mixes can help when our digestive system needs comfort and assistance. Think of blending herbs like ginger, fennel, and peppermint. Fennel promotes digestion and lessens bloating, while peppermint eases indigestion and soothes stomach discomfort. Ginger adds warmth and assists with nausea relief and digestive problems.

Herbal mixes can aid in creating the perfect environment for sleep for a restful night's sleep and a feeling of tranquillity. Combine herbs like chamomile, passionflower, and valerian root. The mild calming effects of valerian root help with relaxation and better sleep. In contrast to chamomile, which is known for its well-known relaxing effects to promote peaceful sleep, passionflower soothes the mind and lessens tension.

Herbal tea blends' diversity and capacity to meet our varying emotions and requirements are what make them so appealing. Herbal teas can elevate our moods, offer comfort, and enhance general well-being in a variety of ways, from encouraging calmness and relaxation to boosting energy and focus. We can make specialized herbal concoctions that address our particular emotional needs by experimenting with various herb combinations. Therefore, the next time you feel down or need a boost of energy, grab for a cup of herbal tea that has been specially brewed for your state of mind and let its mild flavors and therapeutic benefits to calm and enliven your mind, body, and spirit. A toast to the craft of mixing and the pleasure of savoring heavenly brews!

## Healing herbal tea recipes

Herbal teas have long been revered for their curative qualities and the significant effects they have on human health. The craft of making healing herbal tea recipes blends the comfort of a warm cup of tea with the knowledge of nature. We will explore the world of healing herbs in this section and learn about a variety of recipes that help alleviate, nourish, and support a variety of health issues. These medicinal herbal teas offer a natural and comprehensive approach to wellness, with calming mixes for stomach difficulties and immune-boosting infusions.

Our daily lives might be disrupted by digestive problems, but nature provides us with a multitude of herbs that can help us get our digestive systems back in harmony. Combine chamomile, peppermint, and fennel to make a calming tea. While peppermint relieves indigestion and bloating, chamomile soothes the stomach and lessens inflammation. Fennel creates a mild and potent blend for digestive harmony by promoting digestion and easing discomfort.

Herbal teas can act as a natural first line of defense when our immune systems need a boost. Echinacea, elderberry, and rosehip are a few plants you can use to make an immune-boosting mixture. While elderberry is high in antioxidants and supports the immune system, echinacea boosts immunological function and aids in the prevention of infections. Rosehip boosts vitamin C levels, promoting a healthy immune system as a whole. These herbs combine to make a strong concoction that strengthens your body's defenses.

Certain herbs can be quite helpful for supporting the respiratory system and relieving congestion. Thyme, eucalyptus, and licorice root are blended together. Thyme contains antibacterial qualities and relieves congestion and coughs. While licorice root calms the throat and supports healthy respiratory function, eucalyptus serves as a decongestant and provides respiratory support. During times of respiratory pain, this herbal blend offers relief and comfort.

Finding moments of peace and tranquillity in our hectic lives is essential for our wellbeing. Combine herbs like passionflower, lemon balm, and lavender for a calming and stress-relieving tea. While lemon balm provides relaxing qualities that support a sense of well-being, lavender promotes relaxation and lessens anxiety. Passionflower promotes sound sleep and reduces stress. These herbs combine to make a mild and calming blend that calms the body and mind.

Teas made from herbs can boost the body's natural detoxification processes and help with detoxification. Utilize herbs like dandelion, nettle, and burdock root to make a cleansing concoction. Dandelion has diuretic properties that help liver health and detoxification. Burdock root supports liver function and enhances general vigor, while nettle is an excellent source of antioxidants and aids in system cleansing. This herbal blend revitalizes the body and aids with toxin removal.

Numerous health problems can result from chronic inflammation, but some plants have anti-inflammatory qualities that can provide relief. For a calming and anti-inflammatory tea, combine cinnamon, ginger, and turmeric in a blender. Ginger helps with digestion while also reducing inflammation, while turmeric includes curcumin, a potent anti-inflammatory ingredient. Warmth-enhancing cinnamon also helps the body's natural anti-inflammatory activities. The natural and calming solution for lowering bodily inflammation offered by this tea.

Herbal teas can offer mild support and solace to women who are experiencing hormone irregularities. Use herbs like chasteberry, red clover, and dong quai to make a balanced mixture. Chasteberry aids in hormone regulation, easing PMS and menopausal symptoms. Dong quai has been used in traditional Chinese medicine to treat menstruation problems, whereas red clover includes phytoestrogens that may improve hormonal balance. This herbal blend provides balanced hormone support naturally.

Utilizing the healing powers of nature to hydrate, support, and heal our bodies, healing herbal tea recipes provide a holistic approach to wellness. These teas offer a healthy and efficient approach to deal with a variety of health issues, from immune-boosting infusions to calming digestive mixes. We can harness nature's healing powers and improve our general health by including healing herbs into our everyday routines. So, savor the calming warmth of a cup of therapeutic herbal tea and welcome these nature-inspired medicines' nourishing embrace. Toast to a more wholesome and energetic existence!

## Seasonal herbal tea recipes

The tastes, odors, and moods in our environment change with the seasons. Herbal tea is a great way to get in touch with nature and enjoy all that it has to offer while celebrating the beauty of each season. We'll travel through the seasons as we explore a variety of seasonal herbal tea recipes in this section. These dishes will assist us in savoring the essence of each season and forging a stronger bond with the natural world, from the vivid spring blossoms to the comforting winter spices.

Our herbal tea blends can capture the vigor and freshness of the spring season, which is a period of regeneration and reinvigoration. Combine herbs like elderflower, mint, and lemon verbena for a springtime concoction. Mint offers a cool, energizing touch, and elderflower adds a subtle flowery fragrance. Lemon verbena gives a zesty zing that stimulates the senses and blends well with nature's rebirth. This mixture awakens the spirit and captures the spirit of spring.

Warmth, brightness, and a profusion of rich flavors are all brought by summer. Consider combining herbs like hibiscus, lemongrass, and lavender when creating herbal tea recipes for this season. On sweltering summer days, hibiscus has a tart, acidic flavor that is cooling and refreshing. While lavender gives a hint of flowery sophistication, lemongrass adds a zesty flavor and helps with digestion. These herbs combine to make a refreshing and energizing summery combination.

Autumn is a time of change when the scenery takes on magnificent hues and the temperature drops. Consider using herbs like cinnamon, apple, and ginger while developing herbal tea recipes for this season. Cinnamon brings warmth and a touch of spice, making you think of the cozy embrace of fall. Apple adds a pleasant, sweet flavor that goes well with the season's harvest, while ginger gives it a little zing and helps with digestion. This mixture pampers the senses and conjures up the coziness of fall.

Winter encourages us to take things easy, find comfort in warmth, and appreciate the season's delectable flavors. Think about combining herbs like chamomile, peppermint, and cardamom in your winter herbal tea recipes. Long winter evenings are the perfect time to unwind thanks to chamomile's calming qualities. Cardamom gives a sense of spice and warmth, while peppermint adds a cooling and refreshing ingredient. These herbs combine to form a calming and comfortable mixture that celebrates the serenity of winter.

Special herbal tea recipes that embody the joy and enjoyment of the season are required. Use herbs like cranberry, cinnamon, and cloves to make seasonal mixtures. Cranberries have an acidic, tart flavor that is often associated with the season. Cloves offer a hint of aromatic depth, while cinnamon adds warmth and spice. These herbs mix to produce a festive infusion that brings back feelings of celebration and get-togethers.

For special occasions or social gatherings, delicious mocktails can be made using herbal tea recipes. Try different combinations of fruits, herbs, and sparkling water to make hydrating, alcohol-free drinks.

For a colorful and bubbly mocktail, for instance, combine hibiscus tea with fresh berries and a dash of sparkling water. There are countless options that let you make unique mocktails that honor the flavors of the moment.

Seasonal herbal tea recipes are a pleasant way to enjoy the distinctive characteristics of each season and connect with the natural world. These recipes let us delight in the beauty and pleasures that nature delivers, from the vibrant spring blooms to the warm winter spices. We may develop a closer relationship with the environment around us and enjoy the pleasures of embracing the cycles of nature by creating herbal tea blends that capture the essence of each season. So, raise your cup and, one drink at a time, toast to the ever-changing seasons. Toast to the splendor of nature and the sensory experience of seasonally appropriate herbal teas!

# Chapter VII

# Herbal Tea Etiquette and Culture

**Traditional tea ceremonies**

Traditional tea ceremonies provide a peaceful haven where one can discover comfort, awareness, and a deep appreciation for the art of tea in a fast-paced world full of continual distractions. These ceremonies, which are rooted in ancient traditions and rich in symbolism, have been used for centuries by many different nations.

We will set out on a journey to investigate the essence of traditional tea ceremonies, their fascinating history, and the significant effects they have on our emotional, mental, and spiritual health in this section.

Ancient China is where tea ceremonies first appeared because of the medical and spiritual benefits of the beverage. The practice quickly expanded to other Asian countries, such as Japan, Korea, and Taiwan, each of which developed its own distinct tea ceremony traditions. These ceremonies emphasized a holistic approach, embracing mindfulness, aesthetics, and the art of hospitality in addition to tea drinking.

The tea house, a special area created to foster harmony and peace, is a key component in traditional tea ceremonies. Traditional architecture, serene gardens, and minimalist design are common features of tea houses. Every feature of the tea house, from the sliding doors to where the utensils are placed, has a symbolic meaning and invites visitors to enter a sacred realm of calm and mindfulness.

In traditional ceremonies, making tea is a precise and ritualistic process. Each step is carried out with style and intention, starting with the choice of tea leaves and ending with the exact movements of the tea tools and water heating. These traditions place a strong emphasis on mindfulness, urging participants to enjoy the beauty and simplicity of the tea-making process while being fully present in the moment.

Tea brewing is a type of art in and of itself during traditional ceremonies. To get the most flavor and aroma from the tea, the type of tea, water temperature, steeping time, and serving techniques are all carefully picked. The goal is to create an experience that engages all the senses and fosters a deeper connection with the tea and the present moment rather than simply brewing a delicious cup of tea.

Meditation and awareness are embodied in traditional tea ceremonies. Participants are urged to pay attention to the present moment while they take part in the ceremony, taking in the aroma, color, and flavor of the tea as well as the company of others. Participants in this activity can let go of outside distractions and feel a profound sense of calm and tranquillity because it cultivates a state of awareness.

Tea ceremonies are rich with symbolism, and each component has a special meaning. The teapot is a representation of the vessel of life, while the tea leaves stand for harmony and purity. Tea sharing develops a sense of community and connection, and the act of pouring tea reflects respect and humility. These symbols and gestures act as reminders to practice virtues like respect, gratitude, and mindfulness every day.

Different cultures' tea ceremonies have developed in different ways, each reflecting the particular traditions and values of the area. The "Chanoyu" or "Sado," or Japanese tea ceremony, places a strong emphasis on harmony, simplicity, and the appreciation of imperfections. Korean tea rituals emphasize the enjoyment of serene tea gatherings and the aesthetic beauty of tea ware. The art of tea appreciation and the research of many tea kinds are highlighted in Taiwanese tea ceremonies. Understanding these cultural differences helps one better appreciate the many principles and practices related to tea ceremonies.

Traditional tea ceremonies give us a priceless opportunity to calm down, get in touch with our inner selves, and develop harmony and mindfulness. Tea ceremonies offer a break from the hustle and bustle of daily life and allow us to fully immerse ourselves in the transformational power of tea through their rituals, symbolism, and emphasis on the present moment. So, let's respect the historical customs, enjoy each cup slowly, and appreciate the peace that tea ceremonies bring into our life.

## Tea rituals around the world

Tea maintains a particular place in the hearts and rituals of people all around the world. It is a beloved beverage adored by cultures all over the world. Tea has evolved into an essential component of cultural traditions, representing hospitality, connection, and mindfulness in everything from formal ceremonies to daily rituals. In this section, we set out on a journey to investigate the numerous practices, distinctive preparations, and the cultural significance of tea in various regions of the world.

Tea ceremonies have a long history in China, the country where tea was first consumed. The art of steeping tea leaves in little clay teapots is emphasized in the traditional Chinese tea ceremony known as Gongfu Cha. It involves several infusions and emphasizes on the taste, aroma, and texture of tea. The sharing of tea as a sign of hospitality and respect are all represented by the Chinese Tea Ceremony.

In Japan, via the practice of Chanoyu, also known as the Japanese Tea Ceremony or Sado, tea acquires a profoundly spiritual significance. This highly organized ceremony, which has its roots in Zen Buddhism, emphasizes mindfulness, elegance, and simplicity. Matcha, a powdered green tea, is prepared and served in a meditative setting to encourage calmness and a sense of connection to nature.

Moroccans consume tea on a daily basis, and making and serving mint tea has significant cultural significance. Creating a foamy layer by pouring the tea from a height is part of the Moroccan Mint Tea ceremony, which represents the exchange of hospitality and friendship. A representation of Moroccan hospitality, this sweet and energizing concoction of green tea, fresh mint leaves, and sugar is served with a touch of Moroccan flair.

Chai has a particular place in the hearts of the people of India. Chai preparation and drinking serve as a ritual of community and connection that goes beyond simple sustenance. Tea merchants known as "chai wallahs" make strong black tea with milk, flavorings like cardamom, cinnamon, and ginger, and sugar. The tea is boiled, strained, and then poured, creating a lovely sensory experience and encouraging a sense of community.

The British custom of afternoon tea gives the routine of drinking tea style, sophistication, and a hint of luxury. Afternoon tea is a leisurely tradition that dates back to the 19th century and includes a selection of teas, exquisite finger sandwiches, scones with clotted cream and jam, and a choice of pastries and cakes. It's a time for interaction, unwinding, and savoring delicious snacks in a chic environment.

Tea is a major component of social interaction and hospitality in Turkey. Turkish tea, or çay, is made in a unique double teapot called a çaydanlk and is typically served in tiny tulip-shaped glasses. It is enjoyed all day long as friends and family get together to share tales, have conversations, and build relationships. Turkish tea is typically served with a sugar cube on the side and is very strong and black.

Mate, a conventional herbal infusion, is the focal point of the tea ceremony in Argentina. Using a hollowed-out gourd and a metal straw known as a bombilla, a group of friends or family members share mate, a beverage produced from the leaves of the yerba mate plant. The participants' sense of solidarity and friendship are fostered by the ritual of passing the gourd and drinking mate.

Butter tea, also known as po cha, is a common libation and food source in Tibet's highlands. Butter tea, which is made from strong black tea and is combined with yak butter and salt, offers warmth, vigor, and sustenance in the chilly Himalayan environment. The creamy texture of the tea is produced by the churning and pouring technique, and the rich flavor is imprinted in Tibetan tradition.

Worldwide tea ceremonies honor the enduring values of hospitality, connection, and mindfulness. The calming elegance of Japanese tea ceremonies, the lively gatherings around Moroccan mint tea, or the coziness of sharing chai in India are just a few examples of the various ways that tea rituals reflect the distinctive customs, values, and traditions of various countries. By adopting these customs, we can broaden our understanding of tea, create lasting relationships with others, and go on a sensory adventure that crosses boundaries and brings people together through a shared love of this age-old and cherished beverage. So, let's raise our cups, appreciate the tastes, and celebrate the art of tea everywhere.

## Hosting a herbal tea party

An exquisite way to enjoy delicious flavors, celebrate the beauty of nature, and make cherished memories with loved ones is to host a herbal tea party. Such a gathering provides a distinctive and revitalizing experience by fusing the elegance of a conventional tea party with the allure of herbal infusions. In this section, we will discuss the art of throwing an outstanding herbal tea party, from planning and preparation to menu and decor suggestions.

Setting the right mood is essential to throwing a successful herbal tea party. Choose a calm, welcoming location, like a patio, garden, or comfortable living area. To add peace and charm to the space, think of using natural features such as floral arrangements, greenery, and gentle lighting. Pay close attention to how people are seated to ensure comfort and promote conversation.

The selection of superb herbal infusions forms the centerpiece of a herbal tea party. Curate a varied selection of herbs, including well-liked choices like chamomile, peppermint, lavender, and ginger, as well as one-of-a-kind blends that highlight various flavors and fragrances. Allow guests to pick between hot and cold infusions based on their tastes by offering both alternatives. To improve the brewing experience, provide a range of tea accessories, such as infusers and strainers.

Complement the herbal infusions with a meal that was carefully crafted and offers mouthwatering delicacies and delicate snacks. Choose light foods that are energizing and refreshing, such fruit platters, scones, and pastries. Include herbal elements in the menu to give the dishes flavors like lavender, mint, or rosemary. Considering dietary constraints, offer solutions that cater to vegan, gluten-free, or other specialized dietary demands.

Include fun tea-related activities to enhance the experience of the herbal tea party. Set up a tea blending station so guests can select from a variety of herbs and spices to create their own custom tea blends. Make tea tasting notes available and invite visitors to offer their insights. Additionally, to entertain guests and inform them about the world of herbal infusions, think about arranging a tea trivia contest or a quiz with a tea theme.

To improve the entire experience, pay close attention to the aesthetic aspects of the table setting. Pick out sophisticated and themed tea sets, teacups, saucers, and teapots for the gathering. To add a little charm and personality, think about adding vintage or quirky objects. To add a touch of nature to the setting, decorate the table with fresh flowers, herbal sprigs, or tiny potted plants. Make visitors feel special by providing personalized place cards or favors with a tea theme.

To increase the authenticity of the herbal tea party, introduce guests to the customs and etiquette of tea. Introduce the basics of the tea ceremony, such as how to handle teacups properly, how to stir tea in a clockwise motion, and how to pour. Encourage visitors to practice mindfulness, interact with one another, and enjoy each drink of their preferred herbal infusion. The attendees experience a greater appreciation for the tea as well as a sense of relaxation and community as a result of this mindfulness exercise.

Create an environment that encourages interaction between guests to encourage meaningful conversations and connections. Encourage visitors to talk about their favorite teas, their experiences, and their encounters with herbal infusions. Discuss the advantages of herbal tea for your health, cultural customs, or personal experiences. Offering conversation starters or quotes about tea might encourage lively debates and foster a welcoming atmosphere.

By providing tea-themed party favors, you may extend the tea party experience beyond the actual gathering. Think of offering small packages of herbal tea blends, branded tea bags, or souvenirs with a tea theme that visitors can take home as a reminder of the occasion. Put the party favors in nicely adorned bags or boxes and coordinate them with the event's theme. To improve the room's aesthetic appeal, use tea-related décor items like banners or centerpieces in the style of teapots.

A delightful way to enjoy the flavors of herbal infusions, appreciate the beauty of nature, and make enduring memories with friends and loved ones is to host a herbal tea party. You may create a memorable event that stimulates the senses and strengthens connections by putting special emphasis on the atmosphere, meal, activities, and aesthetics. As you set out on this adventure to create an alluring herbal tea party that leaves a lasting impact on your guests, embrace the art of tea and the joy of hosting. Set the scene, steep the tea, and take in the enchantment as it happens with your favorite people.

# Chapter VIII

# Troubleshooting Common Issues

## Bitter or weak herbal tea

Herbal tea is a fascinating beverage with a wide variety of flavors and health advantages. Herbal tea can be unpleasant to drink if it is bitter or weak, which might reduce how much you like the experience as a whole. In this section, we will examine the causes of herbal tea's bitterness or weakness and practical ways to help you make a cup of herbal infusion that is gratifying and well-balanced.

The choice of herbs is one of the main causes of bitterness in herbal tea. Some herbs naturally include substances that add bitterness, such as tannins, alkaloids, or volatile oils. Herbs that can taste bitter include chamomile, valerian root, and several citrus peels. Bitterness can be lessened with careful herb selection that takes into account their flavor profiles.

The temperature and steeping time both significantly affect how herbal tea tastes. The release of bitter compounds can be accelerated by steeping the herbs for an extended period of time at a high temperature. To obtain a balanced flavor profile, it is crucial to follow the suggested steeping periods and temperatures for each herb. It minimizes the release of bitter compounds while enabling the extraction of desired tastes and qualities.

The ratio of the herb to the water is another element that may cause bitterness. An excessive ratio of herbs to water might produce a powerful infusion, which raises the possibility of bitterness. An herbal tea that is tasty and well-balanced can be made by maintaining the right herb-to-water ratio. The perfect balance for any individual herb can be discovered through experimentation and ratio adjustments.

Several factors, starting with the quality of the herbs used, can be blamed for herbal tea's weakness. The flavor and power of the infusion are greatly influenced by the quality and freshness of the herbs. A weak and tasteless tea can be the result of using stale or low-quality herbs. To keep herbs fresh, it is best to get them from reputable suppliers and store them properly.

The strength of a herbal tea is also influenced by the temperature and steeping time. A weak infusion may be the result of insufficient steeping time or brewing at low temperatures. To extract the best flavors and characteristics from a plant, the suggested steeping duration and temperature range should be followed. Herbal tea is powerful and delicious when the temperature and steeping time are balanced properly.

The proportion of the herb to the water can also affect how potent the infusion is. A weak brew can result from using too few herbs in comparison to the water. The flavor and potency of the herbal tea can be improved by adjusting the ratio of herbs to water by adding more herbs.

There are many ways to get rid of the bitterness in herbal tea. Combining different approaches is one practical strategy. To balance the flavors and lessen bitterness, mix bitter herbs with sweeter or gentler plants. Individual blends that suit personal preferences can be created by experimenting with various herb ratios and combinations.

A different solution is to change the temperature and steeping period. Bitterness in herbal tea can be lessened by shortening the steeping time or cooling the water. This method preserves the desirable tastes and characteristics while reducing the production of bitter compounds. To achieve the ideal balance, careful observation and tasting are necessary.

The diluting procedure might be used when the bitterness is excessive. A tiny amount of plain, hot water can be added to soften the flavor and lessen the bitterness. Tea strength and flavor can be precisely controlled by adding small amounts of hot water gradually while tasting.

There are numerous ways to deal with herbal tea's weaknesses. First off, prolonging the steeping period can assist the herbs retain more flavor and power. However, excessive steeping should be avoided as it could result in bitterness. Achieving the proper strength can be aided by keeping an eye on the infusion process and tasting at regular intervals.

Another efficient way to resolve weak herbal tea is to change the proportion of herbs to water. The flavor and intensity of the infusion can be improved by adding extra herbs. It is advised to progressively raise the herb to water ratio until the required strength is attained while making sure a balanced and pleasing flavor.

Last but not least, choosing fresh and high-quality herbs is essential for producing a potent and tasty herbal tea. Using freshly dried or recently gathered herbs guarantees a vibrant and potent infusion.

Herbal tea consumers may be disappointed by bitter or weak tea, but by understanding the causes of these problems, you can avoid them. A well-balanced and enjoyable cup of herbal tea can be made by carefully choosing the herbs, according to suggested steeping periods and temperatures, and modifying the herb-to-water ratio. Additionally, applying the dilution method, modifying steeping conditions, and blending procedures all offer workable solutions for reducing bitterness or weakness. With these suggestions and strategies, you can take advantage of herbal tea's full potential, enjoying its tastes while reaping its health advantages.

# Choosing the wrong herb combinations

Herbal tea is a delightful drink with a wide range of flavors and health advantages. The skill of making herbal tea depends not only in choosing the right herbs individually but also in blending them together to produce soothing flavors and improved characteristics. But selecting the wrong herb combinations might provide unsatisfactory outcomes, impacting the tea's flavor, aroma, and overall experience. The significance of harmonious herb combinations in herbal tea and the potential consequences of choosing incompatible herbs will be discussed in this section. We'll also offer suggestions and recommendations to assist you in selecting the ideal herb combinations for a flavorful and nutritionally sound cup of herbal infusion.

The final flavor, aroma, and medicinal qualities of a herbal infusion can be greatly influenced by the combination of herbs used in its preparation. Each plant has a distinct flavor profile and therapeutic qualities, and when carefully blended, they can provide interesting and satisfying tea blends. The appropriate herb pairings can bring out the desired flavors, strike a pleasing balance, and offer a satisfying sensory experience.

Making herbal tea with the wrong herb combinations can have unfavorable results. Lack of flavor harmony is one of the effects that is most obvious. When combined, certain herbs might overpower other delicate ones because of their strong, dominating flavors. This imbalance may produce a tea that is either overly powerful or lacking in complexity and depth.

Additionally, mixing incompatible herb combinations can result in conflicting aromas. Herbal tea's sensory experience is enhanced by aromatic herbs, but when they are combined incorrectly, the flavors might clash and create an unpleasant or confusing scent profile.

Certain plants have complementary qualities that, when combined, increase the medicinal advantages they provide. However, selecting incompatible herb combinations may negate or lessen these advantages, reducing the tea's intended medicinal effects.

When choosing herb combinations, it's important to keep the following rules in mind to produce a delicious and well-balanced herbal tea:

It's important to comprehend how different herbs taste. While some herbs have more overtly flavorful characteristics, others are more subdued. Take into account how the flavors of the herbs interact and enhance one another while combining them. Before committing to larger quantities, experiment with small batches and taste the resulting mixtures to determine how well the flavors work together.

Think about the medicinal benefits of the herbs and how they can complement one another. Combining certain herbs can increase the potency and efficiency of the tea since they have overlapping or complementary qualities. For instance, chamomile and lavender can be combined to increase the effects of relaxing and sleep promotion.

Focus on the strength of each herb's flavor and strive for a harmonious combination. Herbs with strong flavors should not be combined with those with more delicate flavors. To get the ideal flavor balance, it might be required to experiment with different ratios or change the herb-to-water ratio.

Learn about the traditional combinations and pairings that have been used throughout history. Herbal tea blends have a long history in various cultures and have been produced and perfected over many centuries. Taking ideas from these traditions might give you insightful knowledge about effective herb combinations.

The art of selecting herb combinations for herbal tea ultimately involves experimentation and personal preferences. Try out several combinations and taste them, paying attention to the flavors, scents, and overall experience. To record effective blends and avoid repeating unsuccessful ones, keep a journal of your experimentation.

Let's look at some harmonious blends to demonstrate the beneficial effects of the right herb combinations:

The mixture of chamomile, lavender, and lemon balm is one of the most popular concoctions for calmness and relaxation. The peaceful and aromatic features of lavender blend wonderfully with chamomile's well-known sedative qualities. The use of lemon balm improves the whole experience by adding a mild lemony note. These herbs work well together to produce a calming effect that eases stress and encourages peaceful sleep. After a stressful day, treating yourself to a cup of this soothing herbal tea is the ideal way to relax.

The combination of peppermint and ginger is an effective combination when it comes to promoting digestive health. With its calming and cooling effects, peppermint can help with nausea, bloating, and indigestion. While ginger is renowned for its warming and digestive stimulating properties. These herbs combine to provide an energizing and stimulating tea that promotes digestion, eases discomfort, and calms the digestive system. After a large meal, sipping on a cup of this digestive blend will help you feel better and encourage good digestion.

Combining herbs with potent immunity-boosting characteristics can be quite helpful when immunological support is required. Elderberry, rosehip, and echinacea are widely known for supporting the immune system and acting as antioxidants. The natural defense mechanisms of the body are strengthened by echinacea, while elderberry has antiviral and anti-inflammatory effects. Rosehip, which is high in vitamin C, gives you an extra antioxidant boost. Together, these herbs provide a strong and delicious tea that boosts overall health, supports the body's defenses, and tastes deliciously fruity.

Ginseng, green tea, and lemongrass are common choices for people looking for an energy boost and mental clarity. Ginseng is well-known for its adaptogenic qualities, which maintain vitality and improve cognitive performance. Green tea is a healthy source of caffeine and is high in antioxidants, which help with focus and alertness. Lemongrass enhances the overall flavor profile and offers a revitalizing lemony aroma. This stimulating blend is a great option for individuals who need a mental and physical boost because it not only delivers a natural pick-me-up but also a variety of health advantages.

A delicious and well-balanced cup of herbal tea can only be made by selecting the proper herb combinations. The medicinal effects of the infusion can be enhanced by carefully choosing complementing herbs to complement its aromas and flavors. Tea enthusiasts can develop harmonious blends that provide a pleasurable sensory experience and the desired health benefits by understanding the effects of selecting wrong combinations and adhering to the principles mentioned in this section. So, while you explore the enormous world of herbal tea and its unlimited possibilities for flavorful and healthful herb pairings, let your creativity and curiosity lead the way.

## Storage and shelf-life concerns

Herbal tea has become extremely popular among tea enthusiasts due to its wide variety of flavors and medicinal qualities. Proper storage and consideration of shelf-life are essential if you want to fully appreciate the advantages and flavors of herbal tea. In this section, we'll examine the value of storage techniques, elements that affect herbal tea's shelf life, and best practices for preserving its quality and freshness. Tea enthusiasts can make sure their herbal tea stays fragrant, powerful, and pleasurable for a long time by understanding storage factors.

Herbal tea's quality over time is influenced by a number of factors, including its shelf life. For herbal tea to be properly preserved, it is crucial to comprehend the following factors:

Like any other organic material, herbal tea is vulnerable to air exposure. Oxygen can cause oxidation, which results in the tea losing its flavor, freshness, and aroma. In addition to introducing moisture, exposure to air can also bring bacteria or the growth of mold. It is essential to keep herbal tea in airtight containers with a solid barrier against air to avoid these problems.

Moisture is the enemy of herbal tea. The development of mold, a loss of flavor, and the loss of therapeutic characteristics can all be caused by excessive moisture. Herbal tea needs to be stored dry and away from humidity, condensation, and other sources of moisture in order to be protected from moisture.

Herbal tea's quality can be diminished by light, especially direct sunlight and ultraviolet (UV) radiation. The delicate chemical compounds in the tea may be damaged by light, which will cause the flavor to deteriorate and the color to fade. As a result, herbal tea ought to be kept out of direct sunlight and in a dark atmosphere.

Herbal tea's ability to stay fresh can be negatively impacted by extreme temperatures, both high and low. Low temperatures can result in moisture condensation, which can lead to mold growth or flavor loss, while high temperatures can speed up oxidation and deterioration. To preserve its quality, herbal tea should be kept in a cool place with a constant temperature.

The following best practices ought to be adhered to in order to maximize the quality and freshness of herbal tea:

Herbal tea should be stored in the proper containers, which is essential. Airtight containers provide a great defense against air, moisture, and light. Examples are glass jars with tightly fitted lids and metal tins with sealed closures. The flavor, aroma, and therapeutic qualities of the tea are preserved due to these containers.

To reduce exposure to light and temperature shifts, herbal tea should be kept in a cool, dark location. The best place for storage is a pantry or cabinet away from heat sources. The tea's quality and flavor preservation will be ensured by maintaining a constant temperature.

Herbal tea must be stored in a dry area to preserve it from moisture. Keep it away from areas with high humidity, such the sink, the dishwasher, and the bathroom. Moisture can promote the growth of mold, which would be detrimental to the tea's flavor and health advantages.

It is crucial to correctly label the containers with the name of the herbal tea and the date of purchase or packaging. This procedure aids in keeping track of the tea stock's freshness and rotation. You can use the older teas first and refill the stock with newer batches by keeping note of the dates.

Maintaining the freshness of herbal tea requires limiting exposure to air. Use smaller containers or resealable bags when opening the container to minimize air contact. The aroma, flavor, and potency of the tea are preserved due to this procedure.

To maintain freshness, the herbal tea stock needs to be rotated frequently. Prioritize consuming older teas before adding new batches to the collection. By following this procedure, tea is kept off the shelf for a shorter amount of time, giving you the freshest, most flavorful brews every time.

Herbal tea's freshness, flavor, and quality must be preserved through proper storage and shelf-life management. Tea enthusiasts can enjoy aromatic and flavorful brews for a longer period of time by understanding the factors that affect the shelf-life of herbal tea and putting proper storage methods into practice. The tea's flavor, aroma, and health benefits can be preserved by using correct storage techniques, limiting air exposure, regulating moisture, and maintaining a cool, dark atmosphere. Each cup of herbal tea will provide the desired experience if sensory qualities are consistently monitored and stock is rotated in a suitable manner. Accept these storage recommendations to improve your enjoyment of herbal tea and appreciate the depth of nature's herbal infusions.

## Addressing allergies and sensitivities

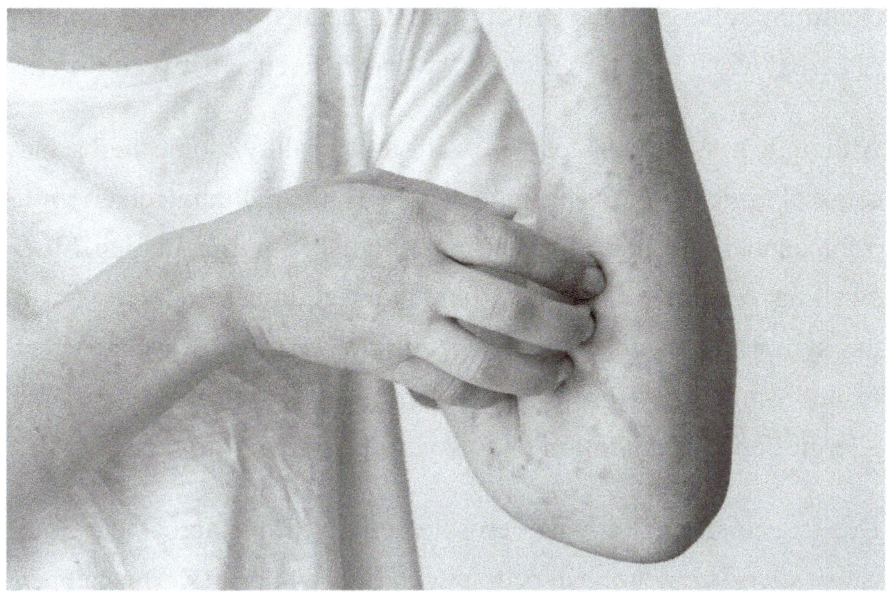

Herbal tea has long been celebrated for its calming effects and other health advantages. However, it is important to approach the use of herbal tea with caution if you have allergies or sensitivities. The topic of dealing with allergies and sensitivities in respect to herbal tea will be discussed in this section. We'll talk about typical allergens, sensitivities, and possible risks related to drinking herbal tea. We'll also offer helpful suggestions and methods for drinking herbal tea responsibly, ensuring that everyone has a great experience.

Sensitivities and allergies are immune system responses to specific substances that the body interprets as dangerous. Allergens like pollen, dust mites, or particular foods cause an instant immunological response, which is what causes allergies. Sensitivities or intolerances, on the other hand, are unfavorable reactions to certain substances that do not involve the immune system but can nevertheless result in discomfort or digestive problems. When examining allergies and sensitivities associated to the consumption of herbal tea, it is important to know the difference between the two.

Although most herbal teas are safe and healthy, some herbs may cause allergic reactions in some people. Herbs including chamomile, mint, dandelion, and echinacea are frequently allergic. Itching, hives, swelling, breathing difficulties, and stomach issues are just a few of the symptoms of an allergic reaction. When ingesting herbal teas made from these herbs, it is important to be aware of these potential allergies and pay attention to how your body reacts to them.

Due to a condition known as cross-reactivity, some herbal teas might cause allergic reactions in people with pollen allergies. This happens as a result of the fact that several plants used to make herbal teas, such birch, ragweed, or grass, are members of the same plant family as typical allergenic pollens. For instance, due to cross-reactivity, people who are allergic to birch pollen may react to chamomile or fennel. For people with pollen allergies to make informed decisions about drinking herbal tea, they must be aware of these possible cross-reactions.

Some people may be sensitive to or intolerant to certain herbal tea ingredients in addition to having allergies. Caffeine, tannins, and certain plants like ginger or peppermint are frequent offenders. Caffeine sensitivity can cause anxiety, jitters, or sleep difficulties. Black teas and other herbal teas include tannins, which might make sensitive people feel uncomfortable with their digestion. It is crucial to be conscious of these sensitivity and select herbal teas that suit your preferences and tolerance levels.

When it comes to allergies and sensitivities to herbal tea, contamination and cross-contamination are possible risks. Instances where allergenic components are additionally processed or stored with the herbal tea can result in contamination and inadvertent exposure. When herbal teas are prepared on utensils that have come into contact with allergic ingredients like milk or nuts, cross-contamination may occur. People who have severe allergies should be extra careful and pick herbal teas from reputable vendors who follow strict manufacturing and labeling guidelines.

With a wide variety of flavors and therapeutic advantages, herbal tea is a source of joy and well-being. However, it is important to approach the use of herbal tea with caution if you have allergies or sensitivities. Let's investigate the methods and procedures to guarantee the secure use of herbal tea. By putting these strategies into practice, people can enjoy the benefits of herbal tea while putting their health and well-being first.

Reading labels and ingredient lists thoroughly is a vital step in safely drinking herbal tea. The contents of a product must be clearly and accurately disclosed by the manufacturer. You can find probable allergens or components that might cause reactions by reading labels. Be mindful of common allergens like nuts, gluten, and soy, and stay away of herbal teas that include ingredients to which you are known to be allergic.

It is highly advised for people with known allergies or sensitivities to seek advice from healthcare specialists. An allergist or dietitian can offer specialized guidance based on your unique requirements and medical background. They can guide you through the different herbal tea selections, point out potential allergens, and make suggestions for substitute herbs or blends that suit your health needs.

It is wise to gradually incorporate a herb or ingredient into your tea practice if you are unsure of your tolerance to it. Start out with modest doses and pay attention to how your body reacts. With this method, you can keep an eye out for any negative effects and plan ahead for future usage. Keep a journal to note your observations and, if necessary, discuss them with your healthcare provider.

Maintaining a line of communication with the staff when purchasing herbal tea from tea shops or cafes is essential. Tell them about any allergies or sensitivities you have, as well as any products or substances you need to stay away from. Staff members who are knowledgeable can answer questions regarding the components of the tea, the dangers of cross-contamination, and provide substitute options that satisfy your needs. You make tea drinking safer by actively participating in these conversations.

Making herbal tea at home gives people with severe allergies or sensitivities more control over the entire process. To reduce the possibility of cross-contamination, think about utilizing specialized equipment such distinct teapots or strainers. Make sure the providers of your ingredients are reputable and free of allergens. You can drink herbal tea with confidence if you follow strict home preparation procedures because you'll know that it meets your own health requirements.

A growing number of tea companies have appeared in recent years with an emphasis on allergen-free or allergy-friendly products. Transparency is a priority for these companies, who clearly label their teas and follow careful manufacturing procedures to avoid cross-contamination. When considering herbal tea choices, look for these brands since they offer further assurance for anyone with allergies or sensitivities.

Consider herbal infusions if you are allergic to or sensitive to any of the typical herbs used in tea blends. Herbal infusions are created from a single herb or plant, as opposed to regular herbal teas, which often include several herbs. This enables you to take advantage of the health advantages of individual herbs without running the risk of allergies or sensitivities brought on by certain mixes.

There are other options to consider if certain allergies or sensitivities restrict your ability to choose from a variety of herbal teas. Think about herbal teas produced with allergen-free components like rooibos, lemon verbena, or lemongrass. Without common allergenic ingredients, these teas have distinctive flavors and medicinal effects.

Herbal tea is typically seen as being risk-free and advantageous, but in order to ensure a pleasant and risk-free tea-drinking experience, allergies and sensitivities must be addressed. Making informed decisions requires being aware of the typical allergies, cross-reactions, and sensitivities related to herbal teas. You can manage your herbal tea intake safely and take advantage of the enticing flavors and health benefits that herbal teas have to offer by adhering to practical suggestions and stating your requirements. Keep in mind that the goal is to enjoy herbal tea while putting your health and wellbeing first.

# Conclusion

## Recap of key points

We have covered a wide range of topics in this e-book that are related to herbal tea, including its definition, how to differentiate it apart from true tea, health advantages, how to choose high-quality herbs, infusion methods, and much more. To strengthen our comprehension and appreciation of herbal tea as we draw closer to the conclusion of our journey, it is helpful to review the major topics raised. This summary will serve as a thorough review of the important topics we have discussed, giving you a complete picture of the herbal tea industry.

### *Getting to Know Herbal Tea:*

As a starting point, we established the term "herbal tea" as an infusion derived from the leaves, flowers, seeds, or roots of numerous plants and herbs. Herbal tea comes in a variety of flavors, scents, and health benefits, unlike true tea, which comes from the Camellia sinensis plant.

### *Differentiating between true tea and herbal tea:*

To fully appreciate herbal tea's distinctive qualities, it is essential to distinguish it from true tea. Although there are many different types of tea, including green tea, black tea, oolong tea, and white tea, herbal tea stands out due to the addition of a variety of herbs, botanicals, and spices.

### *Herbal tea's health advantages:*

We looked into the several health advantages of drinking herbal tea. Herbal teas provide a natural and comprehensive approach to wellness, helping to promote relaxation, ease digestion, and support the immune system and antioxidants.

### *How to Choose High-Quality Herbs:*

We emphasized the need of choosing high-quality herbs in order to offer the finest flavor and medicinal advantages. The entire quality of the herbal tea is influenced by elements like buying from reliable vendors, taking into account organic choices, and keeping an eye on freshness.

### *Techniques for infusion*

We discussed many methods of infusing herbal tea, including steeping, decoction, and cold infusion. Each technique delivers distinctive flavors and qualities that enable unique tea experiences.

### *Proper Storage and Preservation of Herbs:*

Herbs must be stored and preserved in the right ways to maintain their potency and quality. We looked at strategies including keeping herbs in airtight containers, shielding them from light and moisture, and being aware of expiration dates.

*Understanding the Labels on Herbal Tea:*

Consumers can make informed decisions by understanding the labels on herbal tea products. We talked about important label components, such ingredient lists, organic certifications, and allergen warnings, to make tea choosing safer and more individualized.

*Herbs Used Frequently in Herbal Tea:*

We looked at the advantages and characteristics of some of the common herbs included in herbal tea, such as chamomile, rooibos, hibiscus, echinacea, rosehip, and nettle. Each herb has a unique flavor and potential health advantages, which improves the whole tea experience.

*Herbal Tea for Different Purposes:*

Herbal tea can be savored for unwinding, reducing stress, treating certain medical issues, or even as a part of tea ceremonies and rituals. We talked about blending and modifying herbal teas to suit different tastes and demands.

*Pairing Herbal Tea with Food:*

We looked into the method of pairing food with herbal tea to enhance flavors and the entire dining experience. One can build flavorful pairings with various cuisines by learning the flavor profiles and qualities of various herbal teas.

*Herbal Tea Recipes:*

We delved into the world of herbal tea recipes, covering energizing blends, therapeutic blends, seasonal variants, and blends made specifically for various emotions. These recipes offer ideas and directions for making delicious and medicinal herbal tea combinations.

### *Tea Rituals and Ceremonies:*

We looked at the cultural and historical relevance of tea ceremonies and rituals around the world. These traditions—from British afternoon tea rituals to Japanese tea ceremonies—offer a greater understanding of the art of tea and its social and cultural settings.

### *Hosting a Herbal Tea Party:*

We gave advice on how to hold a herbal tea party, including subjects like choosing teas, making accompaniments, and setting up a cozy atmosphere. An enjoyable way to share the pleasures of herbal tea with friends and loved ones is by hosting a tea party.

### *Addressing Allergies and Sensitivities:*

We stressed the significance of taking allergies and sensitivities into account when consuming herbal tea. Individuals are able to make safe and informed decisions while considering other options when they are aware of common allergens, cross-reactions, and sensitivities.

A thorough summary of the herbal tea industry has been given in this section. We have examined its definition, how it differs from true tea, its health advantages, how to choose high-quality herbs, how to infuse them, how to store and preserve them, how to understand tea labels, how to enjoy herbal tea in a variety of ways, including rituals and ceremonies and food pairings. Recapitulating these essential ideas has helped us gain a deeper understanding of herbal tea and all of its potential uses.

Herbal tea is a wonderful and adaptable drink with a variety of flavors, aromas, and health advantages. Herbal tea has a special place in the hearts of all tea lovers, whether it is consumed for unwinding, treating particular health issues, or just as a comfortable and calming beverage. Let's embrace herbal tea's rich history, cultural significance, and the joy it provides to our lives as we continue to learn about it and love it. So let's lift our cups in honor of herbal tea's benefits.

## Encouragement for exploring herbal tea

Herbal tea stands out as a stunning and alluring beverage choice in a world full of a wide variety of beverages. Herbal tea is a fascinating voyage for those prepared to delve into its depths. It is steeped in tradition and is recognized for its numerous flavors and medicinal advantages. The purpose of this section is to inspire and encourage readers to go on their own herbal tea excursions. We can unleash the full potential of nature's infusions and develop a lifelong love affair with this traditional beverage by comprehending the allure, advantages, and versatility of herbal tea.

Herbal tea has a captivating variety of flavors and smells, which is one of its most alluring qualities. Every herb, from calming chamomile to energizing peppermint, adds a distinct flavor to the cup. As we appreciate the varied herbs' delicate floral scents, earthy undertones, and brilliant citrus bursts, we may explore herbal tea as a sensory experience.

A gateway to health and wellness, herbal tea is more than just a tasty beverage. Numerous herbs used in herbal teas are well known for their therapeutic and medical qualities. For instance, ginger has anti-inflammatory qualities, peppermint helps with digestion, and chamomile encourages relaxation. We may use the power of nature to support our wellbeing and foster a holistic approach to health by embracing herbal tea.

Herbal tea helps us re-establish connection with nature and recognize all of its wonderful offerings. As we infuse hot water with the essence of leaves, flowers, seeds, and roots, each cup of herbal tea is a celebration of nature. By learning about herbal tea, we increase our knowledge of and reverence for the plants that live on our earth, cultivating a spirit of gratitude and admiration for the wonders of the natural world.

The ability to customize and develop distinctive blends is one of the delights of herbal tea. We can experiment with combinations and modify scents and flavors to suit our preferences because we have a broad variety of herbs at our disposal. Herbal tea's inventive quality inspires us to experiment, think outside the box, and identify our specific tastes, making each cup a unique expression of who we are.

Herbal tea extends an invitation to slow down, establish rituals, and enjoy peaceful moments. These rituals offer a break from the challenges of daily life, from the quiet morning routine of steeping a cup of herbal tea to the tranquil afternoon pause with a calming infusion. By experimenting with herbal tea, we may incorporate moments of calm and mindfulness into our daily routines, enhancing our wellbeing and building a closer relationship with ourselves.

Around the world, herbal tea is deeply rooted in diverse cultural traditions. Each culture has its own special rituals and beliefs around herbal tea, from the ancient tea ceremonies of Japan to the soothing brews of Ayurveda. Investigating herbal tea allows us to learn more about many civilizations, their history, and their rooted appreciation for nature. By broadening our horizons, this exploration helps us develop a sense of interconnectedness and appreciation for the world.

There are many hidden treasures in the herbal tea industry that are just waiting to be found. With such a wide variety of herbs available, there are constantly fresh flavors and pairings to discover. Rare plants, which captivate our taste senses and broaden our selection of herbal teas, include elderflower, lemon verbena, and butterfly pea flower. We expose ourselves to surprising pleasures and limitless discoveries by moving outside of our comfort zones and trying new herbs.

Herbal tea offers an opportunity for mindful consumption in a hectic and fast-paced world. We become present in the moment as we take our time with each drink and relish it, allowing the flavors and scents to fill our senses. Exploring herbal teas inspires us to develop a conscious approach to consumption, valuing the little things in life and finding delight in them.

Tea made from herbs has a wonderful ability to unite people. Herbal tea develops relationships and a sense of community by facilitating interactions such as brewing a pot of tea with friends and having conversations about herbal remedies and experiences. By learning about herbal tea, we expose ourselves to a thriving and encouraging community of tea enthusiasts, sharing our enthusiasm, information, and experiences with like-minded people.

Exploring herbal tea is a journey full of wonder, flavor, and personal development. By giving in to the allure of herbal tea, we open up a world of flavors, embrace health and wellness, re-establish our connection to nature, and feed our creative side. We find comfort and joy in each cup through rituals, cultural appreciation, and thoughtful consumption. So let's be inspired to explore the world of herbal tea, enjoy what it has to offer, and let its enchantment enrich our lives. Along the way, we learn about the benefits of herbal tea as well as the depths of our own curiosity, creativity, and connection to nature. Cheers to discovering herbal tea's countless delights!

## Final thoughts and future tea adventures

We consider the extraordinary sensations and knowledge gathered over our journey as we come to the end of our exploration into the world of herbal tea. A variety of flavors, scents, and health advantages make herbal tea a flexible and alluring beverage. In the final section, we'll address the value of welcoming new tea experiences, fostering our curiosity, and continuing to broaden our horizons when it comes to herbal tea.

Herbal tea has a broad and dynamic industry. Whether it's a special blend, a unique herb, or a distinct tea culture, there's always something new to learn. By viewing our research of tea as a lifelong journey, we recognize that it is not constrained by the pages of a single book or article. Rather, it is a continuous process of learning, expanding one's knowledge, and developing oneself.

The development of curiosity and openness is one way to maximize the benefits of herbal tea. Every tea encounter should be approached with awe and an openness to trying new flavors and scents. Be willing to experiment with various plants, concoctions, and brewing methods. You open up possibilities for wonderful surprises and enlightening discoveries by adopting a curiosity-driven mindset.

It's fun to create a varied and comprehensive collection of herbal teas. Think about extending your collection by looking for teas from diverse areas, researching herbal remedies from various cultures, and trying unusual flavor combinations. You improve your tea-drinking experience and increase your understanding of herbal teas with each new addition.

Around the world, communities of tea enthusiasts are active and friendly. Participating in these groups offers opportunities for experience sharing, knowledge exchange, and inspiration. Participate in online discussion boards, go to workshops and other tea-related activities, or even host tea parties with like-minded people. You can discover new acquaintances and opportunities for joint tea adventures by engaging with tea communities.

Take the time to learn more about the herbs, their qualities, and their therapeutic advantages as you continue your herbal tea journey. Learn about the traditional tea rituals practiced in numerous cultures throughout the world, explore the scientific studies that support the health benefits of herbal tea, and explore the history and cultural significance of various teas. You gain a greater appreciation for the art and science of herbal tea by broadening your understanding.

It's crucial to embrace sustainability and moral behavior when seeking out tea adventures. Select teas that come from ethical sources that promote fair trade and environmentally sustainable policies. Look for organic certifications, and give priority to teas grown with sustainable farming practices. By making thoughtful decisions, we help to protect the environment and the communities that grow tea.

In addition to being a drink, herbal tea provides an opportunity for calmness and mindfulness. Spend some time developing rituals around your tea-drinking activities. Make sure to intentionally brew your tea, enjoy each drink, and set aside time for introspection. Allow herbal tea to be a regular source of rest, renewal, and inner tranquility.

We are reminded that our tea explorations don't have to come to an end as we say goodbye to this thorough study about herbal tea. Instead, we're urged to keep traveling, discovering new flavors, getting in touch with tea communities, learning more, and appreciating the beauty of herbal tea. Each cup should serve as a doorway to serenity, a source of inspiration, and a motivator for personal development. May we be inspired by awe, an open mind, and an appreciation for the limitless possibilities that herbal tea offers as we set off on future tea journeys. Cheers to a lifetime of discovering tea!

_Thank you for buying and reading/listening to our book. If you found this book useful/helpful please take a few minutes and leave a review on Amazon.com or Audible.com (if you bought the audio version)._